An Introduction to
READING THE APOCALYPSE

Columba Graham Flegg

ST VLADIMIR'S SEMINARY PRESS
CRESTWOOD, NEW YORK 10707
1999

Library of Congress Cataloging-in-Publication Data

Flegg, Columba Graham.
    An introduction to reading the Apocalypse / Columba Graham Flegg.
        p.   cm.
    Includes bibliographical references.
    ISBN 0-88141-131-0 (alk. paper)
    1. Bible. N.T. Revelation Introductions.   I. Title   II. Title: Reading the
Apocalypse
BS2825.5.F54   1999
288'.061—dc21   99-20806
                                                                          CIP

An Introduction to
READING THE APOCALYPSE

Copyright © 1999

St Vladimir's Seminary Press
575 Scarsdale Rd., Crestwood, NY 10707
1-800-204-2665

ISBN 0-88141-131-0

The Scriptural texts are taken from the RSV.

PRINTED IN THE UNITED STATES OF AMERICA

An Introduction to
READING THE APOCALYPSE

Contents

Foreword

In our Christian experience of time and history, we seek to do three things simultaneously: we gather ourselves into the present, we look back, and we look forward. First, we seek to live in the here and the now, entering entirely into "the sacrament of the present moment," discerning the presence of eternity concealed within each moment of time. In the words of St Herman of Alaska, "Let me beseech you, my friends, that from this day onwards, from this hour, from this minute, you will love God above all." We are to love God, the hermit of Spruce Island insists, not at some indefinite point in the past or the future, but in the immediate present: "...from this hour, from this minute..." Then, secondly, we look back to the original blessing conferred on humankind at creation, and to the first coming of our Lord Jesus Christ at his incarnation from the Mother of God. In the third place, we look forward to the End, to Christ's second coming, to the general resurrection and the life of the age to come. Only if we live at one and the same time with full intensity in all these three dimensions—present, past and future—shall we become truly human.

Within the Bible there is one book above all that speaks to us about this third dimension of the End, a book at once inspiring and bewildering, that remains for all too many a closed book, sealed and hidden: the Apocalypse or Revelation of St John. It is a book widely misunderstood, that has given rise to numerous strange heresies; and yet it is a book that we neglect at our peril, for it speaks to us, in the most literal sense, about matters of life and death—eternal life, eternal death. Here, more than anywhere else in Scripture, we recognize the truth of the Ethiopian's reply to Philip: "How can I understand what I am reading, unless someone guides me?" (Acts 8:31).

In Fr Columba Flegg we have found exactly the guide who can help us. For many years he worked at the Open University

in Britain, and his gifts as a teacher are apparent in the clarity
and simplicity with which he writes. He speaks at the same
time as an Orthodox priest, firmly committed to the Tradition
of the Church. Like Fr Pavel Florensky, he is a theologian-
mathematician—which is surely appropriate in a work that is
so full of numbers. His tone is sober and his words are as precise
as possible; and this is of crucial importance when commenting
on a text that has occasioned so much bizarre speculation.
While open to the insights provided by modern biblical scholarship, he takes as his basic guideline the interpretation given
by the Fathers. As we read his pages, gradually we see unfold-
ing before us the coherence of the Apocalypse, the true unity
of its cosmic vision. Here is an introduction to the book of
Revelation that supplements, in a highly illuminating manner,
the commentary by Archbishop Averky of Jordanville.

The Creed ends with an affirmation of future hope: "I look
for the resurrection of the dead..." But the conventional translation "I look for" is far too tame; the Greek has a more dynamic
sense—"I am expecting," "I am eagerly awaiting." The same
note of urgent expectation marks the conclusion of the Apocalypse: " 'Surely, I am coming soon.' Amen. Come, Lord Jesus!"
(Rev. 22:20). Our Christian faith will remain pale and timid unless we also feel this eagerness and urgency in our own hearts.
According to clock time and calendar time the return of our
Lord may seem to be long delayed, but in sacred time it is always near at hand, always imminent. May Fr Columba's study
help all of us to repeat with fresh conviction the early Christian
prayer "Maranatha," "Our Lord, come!" (1 Cor. 16:22).

In my many visits to Patmos, I have often sat alone in the
cave of the Apocalypse, with no sound except the wind outside. Next time I shall take Fr Columba's book with me.

Bishop Kallistos of Diokleia

Introduction

This small work is made up from lectures delivered at a study weekend, February 2-4, 1990, to members of the Orthodox Fellowship of St John the Baptist (the Fellowship of English-speaking Orthodox Christians based in the United Kingdom).

The objective of the lectures was to provide an introduction to the Apocalypse for those unfamiliar with the Book, who wished to read it with some understanding. This work is therefore precisely that—it is not a verse-by-verse commentary, though certain typical passages have been selected for special comment. No wholly satisfactory, detailed Orthodox commentary exists in the English language, and it is therefore to be hoped that one will eventually appear, either as an original work or in translation from another language. For those wishing to read the book with an existing English commentary to assist them, a short bibliography is provided, though the word of warning at the end should be noted.

It is to be hoped that what appears here will stimulate Christians to include the Apocalypse in their regular Bible reading by convincing them of its importance for strengthening their faith and hope in our Lord Jesus Christ—risen, ascended, and glorified, and who shall come again in glory—and in his victory over sin and death. More particularly, the book should forewarn us concerning the seduction of the temptations of the spirit of antichrist which are now all around us and which shall deceive "even the elect." To those who now suffer spiritually or physically in this fallen world, the Apocalypse offers a resounding confirmatory cry of hope and expectation: "Be of good cheer, I have overcome the world."

Father Columba Graham Flegg
Edinburgh 1998

1

1

Old Testament Background

It is important to begin with something about the objectives of this short work and about the way in which its chapters have been planned, hopefully to meet those objectives as far as our restricted space permits.

First, let me emphasize that I do not see this as an academic exercise. Inevitably, it will be necessary to draw on the results of scholarship if we are to come to terms with this remarkable last book of the New Testament. But our major objective, as we study the Apocalypse, is to build up a framework which will help us to read it for ourselves with some degree of genuine understanding of its content. I say "some degree" deliberately, because I cannot make any claim to a complete understanding, nor indeed can anyone else! The book is full of heavenly mysteries. It is the account of a remarkable visionary experience, the meaning of which is still not fully revealed. But it is part of the canon of the New Testament. Without it our Scriptures would be incomplete, and hence our understanding of the Christian faith would be equally incomplete. We cannot, therefore, ignore it. If, at the end of this study, we can turn to the Apocalypse, not as scholars (in the narrow sense of that term), but as ordinary Christian readers, with greater confidence than before, God will have blessed our efforts. Hopefully, we shall be able to read the Apocalypse in a way which will provide us with spiritual sustenance. This will be possible, however, only if we can get behind the imagery to the spiritual meaning which underlies it.

In order to get behind that imagery, it is essential that we be familiar with certain of the prophetic works of the Old Testament, especially the books of Ezekiel and Daniel. There is an extraordinary parallel between Ezekiel and the Apocalypse. It is so striking that a number of commentators have suggested that, in writing the Apocalypse, St John was attempting to provide a Christian version of Ezekiel's prophecy. The actual imagery used, however, is most like that which we find in Daniel, though it is, in fact, also to be found in a number of intertestamental apocalyptic works. In this first chapter, we shall encounter relevant extracts from both Ezekiel and Daniel. It is important that we try to become more familiar than most of us are with the language of Old Testament prophecy, so that such language can be an aid rather than a barrier to our spiritual understanding.

Despite what is written above about this not being an academic exercise, we need to arm ourselves with a little scholarship, to be in a position to read with a critical eye the various introductions to the Apocalypse which we may find in commentaries that we pick up. Such commentaries abound, and the opinions of commentators vary greatly. We need to be on our guard because the Apocalypse has been and will continue to be misused by fanatics of various persuasion. Distortions are made as well by more sober and well-intentioned persons who are in all innocence presenting interpretations which neither serious scholarship nor "orthodox" Christian belief can support. Even today, despite extensive scholarly study, there are still all sorts of hypotheses being put forward about both the authorship of the book and the date of composition. Interpretations of its content range from seeing it as referring only to the specific time of its writing, to its reference being exclusively to the "last days"; or again it is read as providing a history of man's relationship to his Creator from the beginning of time to its end. These matters must be touched upon. In chapter 3, therefore, I shall be saying something about the authorship, dating, and history of the book, as well as about some of the interpretations which are either historically or spiritually significant.

It is perhaps appropriate here to mention one or two of the commentaries which I have myself found helpful, though at the same time I must point out that none can be wholeheartedly recommended. There is, as far as I can tell, only one Orthodox commentary available in English. This is a translation of the Russian Archbishop Averky's commentary, a work which was in turn based largely on the fifth- or possibly sixth-century commentary of St Andrew of Caesarea. This English translation was published (in paperback) by the Valaam Society of America and the St Herman of Alaska Brotherhood in 1985, with the title *Apocalypse*. One of its interesting features is the inclusion of illustrations from an 18th-century Old Believers' manuscript. Of the non-Orthodox commentaries in English, with one exception,[1] the most helpful seem to be by Anglican writers, and I would mention two in particular. First, that by Austin Farrer, published by Oxford University Press in 1964, with the title *The Revelation of St John the Divine*. This is a revised and updated version of an earlier commentary by the same author entitled *A Rebirth of Images*. More recent, and more up-to-date in regard to scholarship, is the commentary by John Sweet in the series of the SCM Pelican paperback commentaries, published in 1979 with the title *Revelation*. There are a number of earlier English commentaries which I have also found useful, such as those by Swete and Charles, but these are difficult to find. There is also a most interesting work by P. Prigent, in French, dealing with the relationship of the Apocalypse to early Christian liturgies, but

1 Richard Baukham, *The Climax of Prophecy* (T & T Clark, 1993), a work of quite exceptional scholarship.

no English translation exists (see the "Short Bibliography"). I must, however, issue a strong "government health warning": some commentaries on the Apocalypse can seriously damage your spiritual health—and, I might add, your intellectual health as well!

Now, if it is important to have some acquaintance with the kind of language used before studying the Apocalypse, it is also essential to have some idea of its overall structure. It does indeed have a structure, though a casual and uninformed reading of it might give some people an impression of general literary chaos. It is not difficult to see that it includes a prologue and an epilogue, and that between these are included four collections of seven items: letters, seals, trumpets, and bowls, together with various short interludes of one kind or another. However, this is too crude a structure for our purposes, and so in chapter 3 I shall also be looking at the structure in more detail, trying to point out some of the problems which arise if we adopt too simple and sequential an interpretation of the various visions. It is only when we have familiarized ourselves somewhat with the language of apocalyptic and obtained some sort of framework for the content of the book, that we can then pass on (as we shall in chapters 4 and 5) to a study of the actual text, devoting a whole chapter first to the "Letters to the Seven Churches." In chapters 4 and 5 we shall study extracts from the actual text. Ultimately, however, I want you to look at it for yourselves in the light of certain questions which are provided for consideration. It is important to emphasize that, although we do not study the text of the Apocalypse itself in this first chapter, its content is extremely important. Without it, we would have to take the symbolic language of the Apocalypse "cold"; and, further, it includes certain passages of Scripture to which later references will be made. It should therefore be read with some care.

There is one further prerequisite crucial for the study of the Apocalypse: that those who study it should be firmly grounded in the essentials of the Christian faith, and, in particular, in "orthodox" Christian eschatological teaching, particularly as it is to be found in the gospels and epistles of the New Testament. We are all well aware that in the Creed, the "Symbol of Faith," we assert our belief that Christ "shall come again in glory to judge both the living and the dead; Whose kingdom shall have no end." As we shall see later, this final phrase was included, specifically because of certain early unacceptable interpretations of the Apocalypse. We also claim in the Creed to "look for the resurrection of the dead and the life of the age to come." Yet what we have in the Creed is only the briefest of summaries of New Testament eschatology; and so, in chapter 2 we shall read Christ's own eschatological teaching as expressed in his "Sermon on the Mount of Olives," often neglected because of his much better known and often quoted "Sermon on the Mount" (which includes the Beatitudes). We shall also read St Paul's eschatological teaching in his epistles to the Corinthians and Thessalonians, together with extracts from epistles of St Peter and St John.

We will take our readings from Scripture in their biblical order. First, let us turn to some passages from Ezekiel. I have already noted that there is a remarkable parallel between this prophetic book and the Apocalypse. Curiously enough, meditation on chapter 1 of Ezekiel (which is included in our first reading) was a recommended way of inducing ecstatic spiritual experience, so you will need to keep your feet firmly on the ground! Notice especially in this first passage the four living creatures, the throne with the glory about it, and the scroll that had to be eaten, all of which we encounter again in the Apocalypse, though we do not find the wheels repeated there.

Ezekiel

Chapter 1

[4]As I looked, behold, a stormy wind came out of the
north, and a great cloud, with brightness round about it,
and fire flashing forth continually, and in the midst of
the fire, as it were gleaming bronze. [5]And from the
midst of it came the likeness of four living creatures.
And this was their appearance; they had the form of men,
[6]but each had four faces, and each of them had four
wings. [7]Their legs were straight, and the soles of their
feet were like the sole of a calf's foot; and they sparkled
like burnished bronze. [8]Under their wings on their four
sides they had human hands. And the four had their faces
and their wings thus: [9]their wings touched one another;
they went every one straight forward, without turning as
they went. [10]As for the likeness of their faces, each had
the face of a man in front; the four had the face of a lion
on the right side, the four had the face of an ox on the left
side, and the four had the face of an eagle at the back.
[11]Such were their faces. And their wings were spread out
above; each creature had two wings, each of which
touched the wing of another while two covered their
bodies. [12]And each went straight forward; wherever the
spirit would go, they went, without turning as they went.
[13]In the midst of the living creatures there was something that looked like burning coals of fire, like torches
moving to and fro among the living creatures; and the
fire was bright, and out of the fire went forth lightning.
[14]And the living creatures darted to and fro like a flash of
lightning. [15]Now as I looked at the living creatures, I saw
a wheel upon the earth beside the living creatures, one for
each of the four of them. [16]As for the appearance of the
wheels and their construction: their appearance was like
the gleaming of a chrysolite; and the four had the same
likeness, their construction being as it were a wheel within
a wheel. [17]When they went, they went in any of their
four directions without turning as they went. [18]The four

wheels had rims and they had spokes; and their rims were full of eyes round about. [19]And when the living creatures went, the wheels went beside them; and when the living creatures rose from the earth, the wheels rose. [20]Wherever the spirit would go, they went, and the wheels rose along with them; for the spirit of the living creature was in the wheels. [21]When those went, these went; and when those stood, these stood; and when those rose from the earth, the wheels rose along with them; for the spirit of the living creatures was in the wheels. [22]Over the heads of the living creatures there was the likeness of a firmament, shining like crystal, spread out above their heads. [23]And under the firmament their wings were stretched out straight, one toward another; and each creature had two wings covering its body. [24]And when they went, I heard the sound of their wings like the sound of many waters, like the thunder of the Almighty, a sound of tumult like the sound of a host; when they stood still, they let down their wings. [25]And there came a voice from above the firmament over their heads; when they stood still, they let down their wings. [26]And above the firmament over their heads there was the likeness of a throne, in appearance like sapphire; and seated above the likeness of a throne was a likeness as it were of a human form. [27]And upward from what had the appearance of his loins I saw as it were gleaming bronze, like the appearance of fire enclosed round about; and downward from what had the appearance of his loins I saw as it were the appearance of fire, and there was brightness round about him. [28]Like the appearance of the bow that is in the cloud on the day of rain, so was the appearance of the brightness round about. Such was the appearance of the likeness of the glory of the Lord. And when I saw it, I fell upon my face, and I heard the voice of one speaking.

Chapter 2

[1]And he said to me, "Son of man, stand upon your feet, and I will speak with you." [2]And when he spoke to me,

the Spirit entered into me and set me upon my feet; and I heard him speaking to me... [9]And when I looked, behold, a hand was stretched out to me, and, lo, a written scroll was in it; [10]and he spread it before me; and it had writing on the front and on the back, and there were written on it words of lamentation and mourning and woe.

Chapter 3

[1]And he said to me, "Son of man, eat what is offered to you; eat this scroll, and go, speak to the house of Israel." [2]So I opened my mouth, and he gave me the scroll to eat. [3]And he said to me, "Son of man, eat this scroll that I give you and fill your stomach with it." Then I ate it; and it was in my mouth as sweet as honey.

In the next passages, notice the promise of judgments upon the very city which was the center of Jewish religion, the evil beasts, the remnant left alive that will escape the sword, the defilement of the holy places by the heathen, and the appearance of the angelic messenger.

Chapter 5

[1]"And you, O son of man, take a sharp sword; use it as a barber's razor, and pass it over your head and your beard; then take balances for weighing, and divide the hair. [2]A third part you shall burn in the fire in the midst of the city, when the days of the siege are completed; and a third part you shall take and strike with the sword round about the city; and a third part you shall scatter to the wind, and I will unsheathe the sword after them. [3]And you shall take from these a small number, and bind them in the skirts of your robe. [4]And of these again you shall take some, and cast them into the fire, and burn them in the fire; from there a fire will come forth into all the house of Israel. [5]Thus says the Lord God: This is Jerusalem; I have set her in the center of the nations, with countries round about her. [6]And she has wickedly rebelled against my ordinances more than the

nations, and against my statutes more than the countries round about her, by rejecting my ordinances and not walking in my statutes. [7]Therefore thus says the Lord God: Because you are more turbulent than the nations that are round about you, and have not walked in my statutes or kept my ordinances, but have acted according to the ordinances of the nations that are round about you; [8]therefore thus says the Lord God: Behold, I, even I, am against you, and I will execute judgments in the midst of you in the sight of the nations... [12]A third part of thee shall die of pestilence and be consumed with famine in the midst of you; a third part shall fall by the sword round about you; and a third part I will scatter to all the winds and I will unsheathe the sword after them. [13]Thus shall my anger spend itself, and I will vent my fury upon them and satisfy myself; and they shall know that I, the Lord, have spoken in my jealousy, when I spend my fury upon them. [14]Moreover I will make you a desolation and an object of reproach among the nations round about you and in the sight of all that pass by. [15]You shall be a reproach and a taunt, a warning and a horror, to the nations round about you, when I execute judgments on you in anger and fury, and with furious chastisements—I, the Lord have spoken—[16]when I loose against you my deadly arrows of famine, arrows for destruction, which I will loose to destroy you, and when I bring more and more famine upon you, and break your staff of bread. [17]I will send famine and wild beasts against you, and they will rob you of your children; pestilence and blood shall pass through you; and I will bring the sword upon you. I, the Lord, have spoken."

Chapter 6

[4]"Your altars shall become desolate, and your incense altars shall be broken; and I will cast down your slain men before your idols. [5]And I will lay the dead bodies of the people of Israel before their idols; and I will scatter your bones round about your altars. [6]Wherever you

dwell your cities shall be waste and your high places ruined, so that your altars will be waste and ruined, your
idols broken and destroyed, your incense altars cut
down, and your works wiped out. [7]And the slain shall
fall in the midst of you, and you shall know that I am the
Lord. [8]Yet I will leave some of you alive. When you
have among the nations some who escape the sword, and
when you are scattered through the countries...

Chapter 7

[23]...and make a desolation. Because the land is full of
bloody crimes, and the city is full of violence, [24]I will
bring the worst of the nations to take possession of their
houses; I will put an end to their proud might, and their
holy places shall be profaned. [25]When anguish comes,
they will seek peace, but there shall be none. [26]Disaster
comes upon disaster, rumor follows rumor; they seek a
vision from the prophet, but the law perishes from the
priest, and counsel from the elders. [27]The king mourns,
the prince is wrapped in despair, and the hands of the
people of the land are palsied by terror. According to
their way I will do to them, and according to their own
judgments I will judge them; and they shall know that I
am the Lord."

Chapter 8

[1]In the sixth year, in the sixth month, on the fifth day of
the month, as I sat in my house, with the elders of Judah
sitting before me, the hand of the Lord God fell there
upon me. [2]Then I beheld, and, lo, a form that had the appearance of a man; below what appeared to be his loins it
was fire, and above his loins it was like the appearance
of brightness, like gleaming bronze. [3]He put forth the
form of a hand, and took me by a lock of my head; and
the Spirit lifted me up between earth and heaven, and
brought me in visions of God to Jerusalem, to the
entrance of the gateway of the inner court that faces
north, where was the seat of the image of jealousy, which

provokes to jealousy. [4]And behold, the glory of the God of Israel was there, like the vision that I saw in the plain.

Notice next the marking of those who are to be spared, the sapphire stone like a throne, the taking of coals of fire from between the cherubim, the filling of the house with the cloud, and the further reference to the glory of God above the cherubim.

Chapter 9

[4]And the Lord said to him, "Go through the city, through Jerusalem, and put a mark upon the foreheads of the men who sigh and groan over all the abominations that are committed in it." [5]And to the others he said in my hearing, "Pass through the city after him, and smite; your eye shall not spare, and you shall show no pity; [6]slay old men outright, young men and maidens, little children and women, but touch no one upon whom is the mark. And begin at my sanctuary." So they began with the elders who were before the house.

Chapter 10

[1]Then I looked, and, behold, on the firmament that was over the heads of the cherubim there appeared above them something like a sapphire, in form resembling a throne. [2]And he said to the man clothed in linen, "Go in among the whirling wheels underneath the cherubim; fill your hands with burning coals from between the cherubim, and scatter them over the city." And he went in before my eyes. [3]Now the cherubim were standing on the south side of the house, when the man went in; and a cloud filled the inner court. [4]And the glory of the Lord went up from the cherubim to the threshold of the house; and the house was filled with the cloud, and the court was full of the brightness of the glory of Lord. [5]And the sound of the wings of the cherubim was heard as far as the outer court, like the voice of God Almighty when he speaks. [6]And when he commanded the man clothed in linen, "Take fire from between the whirling wheels,

from between the cherubim," he went in and stood beside a wheel. [7]And a cherub stretched forth his hand from between the cherubim to the fire that was between the cherubim, and took some of it, and put it into the hands of the man clothed in linen, who took it and went out. [8]The cherubim appeared to have the form of a human hand under their wings. [9]And I looked, and behold, there were four wheels beside the cherubim, one beside each cherub; and the appearance of the wheels was like sparkling chrysolite. [10]And as for their appearance, the four had the same likeness, as if a wheel were within a wheel. [11]When they went, they went in any of their four directions without turning as they went... [12]And their rims, and their spokes, and the wheels were full of eyes round about—the wheels that the four of them had... [14]And every one had four faces: the first face was the face of the cherub, and the second face was the face of a man, and the third the face of a lion, and the fourth the face of an eagle. [15]And the cherubim mounted up. These were the living creatures that I saw by the river Chebar. [16]And when the cherubim went, the wheels went beside them; and when the cherubim lifted up their wings to mount up from the earth, the wheels did not turn from beside them. [17]When they stood still, these stood still, and when they mounted up, these mounted up with them; for the spirit of the living creature was in them. [18]Then the glory of the Lord went forth from the threshold of the house, and stood over the cherubim. [19]And the cherubim lifted up their wings, and mounted up from the earth in my sight as they went forth, with the wheels beside them; and they stood at the door of the east gate of the house of the Lord; and the glory of the God of Israel was over them.

Notice now the beloved of the Lord who has become the harlot, an adulterer with the world around, and God's judgment to be carried out by those with whom the harlot has committed fornication.

Chapter 16

[8]"When I passed by you again and looked upon you, behold, you were at the age for love; and I spread my skirt over you, and covered your nakedness: yet, I plighted my troth to you, and entered into a covenant with you, says the Lord God, and you became mine. [9]Then I bathed you with water and washed off your blood from you, and anointed you with oil. [10]I clothed you also with embroidered cloth and shod you with leather, I swathed you in fine linen, and covered you with silk. [11]And I decked you with ornaments, and put bracelets on your arms, and a chain on your neck. [12]And I put a ring on your nose, and earrings in your ears, and a beautiful crown upon your head. [13]Thus you were decked with gold and silver; and your raiment was of fine linen, and silk, and embroidered cloth; you ate fine flour and honey and oil. You grew exceedingly beautiful, and came to regal estate. [14]And your renown went forth among the nations for your beauty, for it was perfect through the splendor which I had bestowed upon you, says the Lord God. [15]"But you trusted in your beauty, and played the harlot because of your renown, and lavished your harlotries on any passer-by. [16]You took some of your garments, and made for yourself gaily decked shrines, and on them played the harlot; the like has never been, nor ever shall be. [17]You also took your fair jewels of my gold and of my silver, which I had given you, and made for yourself images of men, and with them played the harlot... [23]And after all thy wickedness (woe, woe to you! says the Lord God), [24]you built yourself a vaulted chamber, and made yourself a lofty place in every square; [25]at the head of every street you built your lofty place and prostituted your beauty, offering yourself to any passer-by, and multiplying your harlotry. [26]You also played the harlot with the Egyptians, your lustful neighbors, multiplying your harlotry, to provoke me to anger. [27]Behold, therefore, I stretched out my hand against you, and diminished your allotted portion, and

delivered you to the greed of your enemies, the daughters of the Philistines, who are ashamed of your lewd behavior. [28]You played the harlot also with the Assyrians, because you were insatiable; yea, you played the harlot with them, and still you were not satisfied. [29]You multiplied your harlotry also with the trading land of Chalde'a; and even with this you were not satisfied. [30]How lovesick is your heart, says the Lord God, seeing you did all these things, the deeds of a brazen harlot; [31]building your vaulted chamber at the head of every street, and making your lofty place in every square. Yet you were not like a harlot, because you scorned hire. [32]Adulterous wife, who receives strangers instead of her husband!... [35]Wherefore, O harlot, hear the word of the Lord: [36]Thus says the Lord God, Because your shame was laid bare and your nakedness uncovered in your harlotry with your lovers, and because of all your idols, and because of the blood of your children that you gave to them, [37]therefore, behold, I will gather all your lovers, with whom you took pleasure, all those you loved and all those you loathed; I will gather them against you from every side, and will uncover your nakedness to them, that they may see all your nakedness. [38]And I will judge you as women who break wedlock and shed blood are judged, and bring upon you the blood of wrath and jealousy. [39]And I will give you into the hand of your lovers, and they shall throw down your vaulted chamber and break down your lofty places; they shall strip you of your clothes and take your fair jewels, and leave you naked and bare. [40]They shall bring up a host against you, and they shall stone you, and cut you to pieces with their swords. [41]And they shall burn your houses and execute judgments upon you in the sight of many women; I will make you stop playing the harlot, and you shall also give hire no more."

Notice next the destruction of Tyre and the lamentation over it (which is paralleled in the Apocalypse by the fall of Babylon and the lament over it).

Chapter 27

[1]The word of the Lord came to me: [2]"Now you, son of man, raise a lamentation over Tyre, [3]and say to Tyre, who dwells at the entrance to the sea, merchant of the peoples on many coastlands, thus says the Lord God: O Tyre, you have said, 'I am perfect in beauty.' [4]Your borders are in the heart of the seas; your builders made perfect your beauty."

Chapter 28

[3]...you are indeed wiser than Daniel; no secret is hidden from you; [4]by your wisdom and your understanding you have gotten wealth for yourself, and have gathered gold and silver into your treasuries; [5]by your great wisdom in trade you have increased your wealth, and your heart has become proud in your wealth—[6]therefore thus says the Lord God: "Because you consider yourself as wise as a god, [7]therefore, behold, I will bring strangers upon you, the most terrible of the nations; and they shall draw their swords against the beauty of your wisdom and defile your splendor. [8]They shall thrust you down into the Pit, and you shall die the death of the slain in the heart of the seas." [11]Moreover the word of the Lord came to me: [12]"Son of man, raise a lamentation over the king of Tyre, and say to him, Thus says the Lord God: 'You were the signet of perfection, full of wisdom and perfect in beauty. [13]You were in Eden, the garden of God; every precious stone was your covering, carnelian, topaz, and jasper, chrysolite, beryl, and onyx, sapphire, carbuncle, and emerald; and wrought in gold were your settings and your engravings. On the day that you were created they were prepared. [14]With an anointed guardian cherub I placed you; you were on the holy mountain of God; in the midst of the stones of fire you walked. [15]You were blameless in your ways from the day you were created, till iniquity was found in you. [16]In the abundance of your trade you were filled with violence, and you sinned; so I cast you as a profane thing from the mountain of

God, and the guardian cherub drove you out from the midst of the stones of fire. [17]Your heart was proud because of your beauty; you corrupted your wisdom for the sake of your splendor. I cast you to the ground; I exposed you before kings, to feast their eyes on you. [18]By the multitude of your iniquities, in the unrighteousness of your trade you profaned your sanctuaries; so I brought forth fire from the midst of you; it consumed you, and I turned you to ashes upon the earth in the sight of all who saw you. [19]All who know you among the peoples are appalled at you; you have come to a dreadful end and shall be no more for ever."

We will not include the vision of the valley of dry bones, which must be familiar to you (and which has its counterpart in the resurrection passages in the Apocalypse), but go on to the introduction of Gog and Magog, noting their enacting of God's judgments upon Israel, the birds which consume the dead, the limitation upon the duration of the tribulations, and the recognition of God by the heathen because of His judgments upon unfaithful Israel.

Chapter 38

[1]The word of the Lord came to me: [2]"Son of man, set your face toward Gog, of the land of Magog, the chief prince of Meshech and Tubal, and prophesy against him [3]and say, Thus says the Lord God: Behold, I am against you, O Gog, chief prince of Meshech and Tubal; [4]and I will turn you about, and put hooks into your jaws, and I will bring you forth, and all your army, horses and horsemen, all of them clothed in full armor, a great company with buckler and shield, wielding swords... [8]After many days you will be mustered; in the latter years you will go against the land that is restored from war, the land where people were gathered from many nations upon the mountains of Israel, which had been a continual waste; its people were brought out from the nations and now dwell securely, all of them. [9]You will advance, coming on like

a storm, you will be like a cloud covering the land, you and all your hordes, and many peoples with you... [15]and come from your place out of the uttermost parts of the north, you and many peoples with you, all of them riding on horses, a great host, a mighty army; [16]you will come up against my people Israel, like a cloud covering the land. In the latter days I will bring you against my land, that the nations may know me, when through you, O Gog, I vindicate my holiness before their eyes. [17]Thus says the Lord God: Are you he of whom I spoke in former days by my servants the prophets of Israel, who in those days prophesied for years that I would bring you against them? [18]But on that day, when Gog shall come against the land of Israel, says the Lord God, my wrath will be roused. [19]For in my jealousy and in my blazing wrath I declare, On that day there shall be a great shaking in the land of Israel; [20]the fish of the sea, and the birds of the air, and the beasts of the field, and all creeping things that creep on the ground, and all the men that are upon the face of the earth, shall quake at my presence, and the mountains shall be thrown down, and the cliffs shall fall, and every wall shall tumble to the ground. [21]I will summon every kind of terror against Gog, says the Lord God; every man's sword will be against his brother. [22]With pestilence and bloodshed I will enter into judgment with him; and I will rain upon him and his hordes and the many peoples that are with him, torrential rains and hailstones, fire, and brimstone. [23]So I will show my greatness and my holiness and make myself known in the eyes of many nations. Then they will know that I am the Lord."

Chapter 39

[4]"You shall fall upon the mountains of Israel, you and all your hordes and the peoples that are with you; I will give you to birds of prey of every sort and to the wild beasts to be devoured. [5]You shall fall in the open field; for I have spoken, says the Lord God. [6]And I will send fire on

Magog and those who dwell securely in the coastlands;
and they shall know that I am the Lord. [7]And my holy
name I will make known in the midst of my people Israel;
and I will not let my holy name be profaned any more; and
the nations shall know that I am the Lord, the Holy One in
Israel... [11]On that day I will give to Gog a place for
burial in Israel, the Valley of the Travelers east of the
sea; it will block the travelers, for there Gog and all his
multitude will be buried; it will be called the valley of
Hamon-gog. [12]For seven months the house of Israel will
be burying them, in order to cleanse the land. [13]All the
people of the land will bury them; and it will redound to
their honor on the day that I show my glory, says the
Lord God... [21]And I will set my glory among the nations; and all the nations shall see my judgment which I
have executed, and my hand which I have laid on them.
[22]The house of Israel shall know that I am the Lord their
God, from that day forward. [23]And the nations shall
know that the house of Israel went into captivity for
their iniquity, because they dealt treacherously with me
that I hid my face from them and gave them into the hand
of their adversaries, and they all fell by the sword. [24]I
dealt with them according to their uncleanness and their
transgressions, and hid my face from them."

Finally in Ezekiel, we should note the man with a measuring reed, the healing waters proceeding from the sanctuary,
and the gates named after the twelve tribes. Above all, we
should note the vision of the holy city in which God dwells (so
much a feature of the Apocalypse), but here with its temple (by
contrast absent from the Apocalypse, whose Holy City needs
no temple in it). This is significant, as Jewish apocalyptic writing was primarily directed to the establishment of a kingdom
on earth where the temple would be needed. Christian hopes,
however, are directed toward a kingdom "not of this world," in
which no temple is needed because the whole kingdom is the
seat of God's presence.

Chapter 40

[2]...and brought me in the visions of God into the land of Israel, and set me down upon a very high mountain, on which was a structure like a city opposite me. [3]When he brought me there, behold, there was a man, whose appearance was like bronze, with a line of flax and a measuring reed in his hand; and he was standing in the gateway. [4]And the man said unto me, "Son of man, look with your eyes, and hear with your ears, and set your mind upon all that I shall show you, for you were brought here in order that I might show it to you; declare all that you see to the house of Israel." [5]And behold, there was a wall all around the outside of the temple area, and the length of the measuring reed in the man's hand was six long cubits, each being a cubit and a handbreadth in length; so he measured the thickness of the wall, one reed; and the height, one reed. [6]Then he went into the gateway facing east, going up its steps, and measured the threshold of the gate, one reed deep;... [20]and behold, there was a gate which faced toward the north, belonging to the outer court. He measured its length and its breadth... [24]And he led me toward the south, and behold, there was a gate on the south; and he measured its jambs and its vestibule; they had the same size as the others... [35]Then he brought me to the north gate, and he measured it; it had the same size as the others.

Chapter 43

[1]Afterward he brought me to the gate, the gate facing east. [2]And behold, the glory of the God of Israel came from the east; and the sound of his coming was like the sound of many waters; and the earth shone with his glory... [4]As the glory of the Lord entered the temple by the gate facing east, [5]the Spirit lifted me up, and brought me into the inner court; and behold, the glory of the Lord filled the temple. [6]While the man was standing beside me, I heard one speaking to me out of the temple; [7]and he said to me, "Son of man, this is the place of my throne

and the place of the soles of my feet, where I will dwell in the midst of the people of Israel for ever. And the house of Israel shall no more defile my holy name, neither they, nor their kings, by their harlotry, and by the dead bodies of their kings, [8]by setting their threshold by my threshold and their doorposts beside my doorposts, with only a wall between me and them. They have defiled my holy name by their abominations which they have committed, so I have consumed them in my anger. [9]Now let them put away their idolatry and the dead bodies of their kings far from me, and I will dwell in their midst for ever."

Chapter 47

[1]Then he brought me back to the door of the temple; and behold, water was issuing from below the threshold of the temple toward the east (for the temple faced east); and the water was flowing down from below the south end of the threshold of the temple, south of the altar. [2]Then he brought me out by way of the north gate, and led me round on the outside to the outer gate, that faces toward the east; and the water was coming out on the south side... [8]And he said to me, "This water flows toward the eastern region and goes down into the Arabah; and when it enters the stagnant waters of the sea, the water will become fresh. [9]And wherever the river goes every living creature which swarms, will live, and there will be very many fish; for this water goes there, that the waters of the sea may become fresh; so everything will live where the river goes."

Chapter 48

[30]"These shall be the exits of the city: On the north side, which is to be four thousand five hundred cubits by measure, [31]three gates, the gate of Reuben, the gate of Judah, and the gate of Levi, the gates of the city being named after the tribes of Israel. [32]On the east side, which is to be four thousand five hundred cubits, three gates, the gate of Joseph, the gate of Benjamin, and the

gate of Dan. ³³On the south side, which is to be four thousand five hundred cubits by measure, three gates, the gate of Simeon, the gate of Is'sachar, and the gate of Zeb'ulun. ³⁴On the west side, which is to be four thousand five hundred cubits, three gates, the gate of Gad, the gate of Asher, and the gate of Naph'tali. ³⁵The circumference of the city shall be eighteen thousand cubits. And the name of the city henceforth shall be, The Lord is there."

All these things that we have been noting in these readings reappear in the Apocalypse more or less in the same order. It is small wonder, therefore, that some commentators have described the Apocalypse as a "Christian Ezekiel."

Daniel

Now we turn to the book of Daniel, where the kind of language used is even closer to that of the Apocalypse. We read first about Nebuchadnezzar's dream. Note especially the application of the vision to actual worldly kingdoms (or empires) and the promise of a kingdom that shall not be destroyed. Note too that four kingdoms are spoken of. Four is the significant number in apocalyptic (and other) biblical writings. It represents the whole earth, which has four winds, four seasons, and is said also to have four corners. In this first passage, the king's dream has been revealed by God to Daniel, who declares it to him together with its interpretation.

Chapter 2

³¹You saw, O king, and behold, a great image. This image, mighty and of exceeding brightness, stood before you, and its appearance was frightening. ³²The head of this image was of fine gold, its breast and arms of silver, its belly and thighs of bronze, ³³its legs of iron, its feet partly of iron and partly of clay. ³⁴As you looked, a stone was cut out by no human hand, and it smote the image on its feet of iron and clay, and broke them in pieces;

[35]then the iron, the clay, the bronze, the silver, and the gold, all together were broken in pieces, and became like the chaff of the summer threshing floors; and the wind carried them away, so that no trace of them could be found. But the stone that struck the image became a great mountain, and filled the whole earth. [36]This was the dream; now we will tell the king its interpretation. [37]You, O king, the king of kings, to whom the God of heaven has given the kingdom, the power, and the might, and the glory, [38]and into whose hand he has given, wherever they dwell, the sons of men, the beasts of the field and the birds of the air, making you rule over them all—you are the head of gold. [39]After you shall arise another kingdom inferior to you, and yet a third kingdom of bronze, which shall rule over all the earth. [40]And there shall be a fourth kingdom, strong as iron, because iron breaks to pieces and shatters all things; and like iron which crushes, it shall break and crush all these. [41]And as you saw the feet and toes partly of potter's clay and partly of iron, it shall be a divided kingdom; but some of the firmness of iron shall be in it, just as you saw iron mixed with the miry clay. [42]And as the toes of the feet were partly iron and partly clay, so the kingdom shall be partly strong and partly brittle. [43]As you saw the iron mixed with miry clay, so they will mix with one another in marriage, but they will not hold together, just as iron does not mix with clay. [44]And in the days of those kings the God of heaven will set up a kingdom which shall never be destroyed, nor shall its sovereignty be left to another people. It shall break in pieces all these kingdoms and bring them to an end, and it shall stand for ever..."

Next we turn to Daniel's dream of the four great beasts which come out of the sea. Again, note the number four and the application to four kingdoms or empires. Note too the significance given to the horns of the beasts, and the final reference to judgment and the kingdom of the saints. All this is echoed in the Apocalypse.

Chapter 7

¹In the first year of Belshaz'zar king of Babylon, Daniel had a dream and visions of his head as he lay in his bed. Then he wrote down the dream, and told the sum of the matter. ²Daniel said, "I saw in my vision by night, and behold, the four winds of heaven were stirring up the great sea. ³And four great beasts came up out of the sea, different from one another. ⁴The first was like a lion and had eagles' wings. Then as I looked its wings were plucked off, and it was lifted up from the ground and made to stand upon two feet like a man; and the mind of a man was given to it. ⁵And behold, another beast, a second one, like a bear. It was raised up on one side; it had three ribs in its mouth between its teeth; and it was told, 'Arise, devour much flesh.' ⁶After this I looked, and lo, another, like a leopard, with four wings of a bird on its back; and the beast had four heads; and dominion was given to it. ⁷After this I saw in the night visions, and behold, a fourth beast, terrible and dreadful and exceedingly strong; and it had great iron teeth; it devoured and broke in pieces, and stamped the residue with its feet. It was different from all the beasts that were before it; and it had ten horns. ⁸I considered the horns, and behold, there came up among them another horn, a little one, before which three of the first horns were plucked up by the roots; and behold, in this horn were eyes like the eyes of a man, and a mouth speaking great things. ⁹As I looked, thrones were placed and one that was ancient of days took his seat; his raiment was white as snow, and the hair of his head like pure wool; his throne was fiery flames, its wheels were burning fire. ¹⁰A stream of fire issued and came forth from before him; thousand thousands served him, and ten thousand times ten thousand stood before him; the court sat in judgment, and the books were opened. ¹¹I looked then because of the sound of the great words which the horn was speaking. And as I looked, the beast was slain, and its body destroyed and given over to be burned with fire. ¹²As for the rest of the

beasts, their dominion was taken away, but their lives were prolonged for a season and a time. [13]I saw in the night visions, and behold, with the clouds of heaven there came one like a son of man, and he came to the Ancient of Days and was presented before him. [14]And to him was given dominion and glory and kingdom, that all peoples, nations, and languages, should serve him; his dominion is an everlasting dominion, which shall not pass away, and his kingdom one that shall not be destroyed. [15]As for me, Daniel, my spirit within me was anxious and the visions of my head alarmed me. [16]I approached one of those who stood there, and asked him the truth concerning all this. So he told me, and made known to me the interpretation of the things. [17]'These four great beasts are four kings who shall arise out of the earth. [18]But the saints of the Most High shall receive the kingdom, and possess the kingdom for ever, for ever and ever.' [19]Then I desired to know the truth concerning the fourth beast, which was different from all the rest, exceedingly terrible, with its teeth of iron and claws of bronze; and which devoured and broke in pieces, and stamped the residue with its feet; [20]and concerning the ten horns that were on its head, and the other which came up and before which three of them fell; the horn which had eyes and a mouth that spoke great things, and which seemed greater than its fellows. [21]As I looked, this horn made war with the saints, and prevailed over them, [22]until the Ancient of Days came, and judgment was given for the saints of the Most High, and the time came when the saints received the kingdom. [23]Thus he said, 'As for the fourth beast, there shall be a fourth kingdom on earth, which shall be different from all the kingdoms, and it shall devour the whole earth, and trample it down, and break it to pieces. [24]As for the ten horns, out of this kingdom ten kings shall arise, and another shall arise after them; he shall be different from the former ones, and shall put down three kings. [25]He shall speak words against the Most High, and shall wear out the saints of the Most High,

and shall think to change the times and the law; and they
shall be given into his hand for a time, two times, and
half a time. [26]But the court shall sit in judgment, and his
dominion shall be taken away, to be consumed and destroyed to the end. [27]And the kingdom and the dominion
and the greatness of the kingdoms under the whole
heaven shall be given to the people of the saints of the
Most High; their kingdom shall be an everlasting kingdom, and all dominions shall serve and obey them.'

In the next passage, horns again assume great significance,
here representing actual rulers. Note that we have a saint asking
how long the sanctuary will be trodden underfoot and a reply
indicating that it will be only for a fixed period. Again we have
reference to four kingdoms following that of Greece (i.e. the
empire of Alexander the Great). Note that the vision is specifically related to the time of the end when a particularly dark and
fierce destroyer-king appears who magnifies himself through
craft, opposes the Prince of princes, but who is eventually broken. Finally, note the phrase "the evening and the morning."
This always relates to a period within time, though not necessarily limited to twenty-four hours. The eschatological day,
never limited to a fixed period of time, is always described as
"the morning and the evening." It has no night!

Chapter 8

[3]I raised my eyes and saw, and behold, a ram standing on
the bank of the river. It had two horns; and both horns
were high, but on was higher than the other, and the
higher one came up last. [4]I saw the ram charging west-
ward and northward and southward; no beast could stand
before him, and there was no one who could rescue from
his power; he did as he pleased and magnified himself.
[5]As I was considering, behold, a he-goat came from the
west across the face of the whole earth, without touching
the ground; and the goat had a conspicuous horn between
his eyes. [6]He came to the ram with the two horns, which

I had seen standing on the bank of the river, and he ran at him in his mighty wrath. [7]I saw him come close to the ram, and he was enraged against him and struck the ram and broke his two horns; and the ram had no power to stand before him, but he cast him down to the ground and trampled upon him; and there was no one who could rescue the ram from his power. [8]Then the he-goat magnified himself exceedingly; but when he was strong, the great horn was broken, and instead of it came up four conspicuous horns toward the four winds of heaven. [9]Out of one of them came forth a little horn, which grew exceedingly great toward the south, toward the east, and toward the glorious land. [10]It grew great, even to the host of heaven; and some of the host of the stars it cast down to the ground, and trampled upon them. [11]It magnified itself, even up to the Prince of the host; and the continual burnt offering was taken away from him, and the place of his sanctuary was overthrown. [12]And the host was given over to it together with the continual burnt offering through transgression; and truth was cast down the to the ground and the horn acted and prospered. [13]Then I heard a holy one speaking; and another holy one said to the one that spoke, "For how long is the vision concerning the continual burnt offering, the transgression that makes desolate, and the giving over of the sanctuary and host to be trampled under foot?" [14]And he said to him, "For two thousand and three hundred evenings and mornings; then the sanctuary shall be restored to its rightful state." [15]When I, Daniel, had seen the vision, and sought to understand it; and behold, there stood before me one having the appearance of a man. [16]And I heard a man's voice between the banks of the U'lai, and it called, "Gabriel, make this man understand the vision." [17]So he came near where I stood; and when he came, I was frightened and fell upon my face. But he said to me, "Understand, O son of man that the vision is for the time of the end." [18]As he was speaking to me, I fell into a deep sleep with my face to the ground; but he touched me, and set me on my feet. ¹⁹He said, "Behold, I will make known to you what shall be at the latter end of the indignation; for it pertains to the appointed time of the end. ²⁰As for the ram which you saw with two horns, these are the kings of Media and Persia. ²¹And the he-goat is the king of Greece; and the great horn between his eyes is the first king. ²²As for the horn that was broken, in place of which four others arose, four kingdoms shall arise from his nation, but not with his power. ²³And at the latter end of their rule, when the transgressors have reached their full measure, a king of bold countenance, one who understands riddles, shall arise. ²⁴His power shall be great, and he shall cause fearful destruction, and shall succeed in what he does, and destroy mighty men and the people of the saints. ²⁵By his cunning he shall make deceit prosper under his hand, and in his own mind he shall magnify himself. Without warning he shall destroy many; he shall even rise up against the Prince of princes, but, by no human hand, he shall be broken. ²⁶The vision of the evenings and the mornings which has been told is true; but seal up the vision, for it pertains to many days hence."

In our last passage from Daniel we find a reference to the Archangel Michael, supporting God's children in the time of supreme trouble. There is mention of names in a book introducing a resurrection passage. We again encounter the river, the question "How long?" and the significant limited period, here "a time, two times and half a time," that is, a half-week of days or possibly years. The day-year relationship occurs frequently in biblical texts, and a half-week is especially significant for the Apocalypse. If a day is read as a year, then we have a period of 1260 days, that is, a year of 360 days, plus two such years and half a year. Three-and-a-half is half of seven, the number signifying completeness. It is four, plus three, the number of God. Creation was completed in six days, which were followed by a day of rest, making seven in all. (The eschatological day, to which I have already referred, is [symbolically] the eighth day.) Note finally that the prophecy is sealed until the end time, and that there is a final blessing on those who wait.

Chapter 12

[1]"At that time shall arise Michael, the great prince who has charge of your people. And there shall be a time of trouble, such as never has been since there was a nation till that time; but at that time your people shall be delivered, every one whose name shall be found written in the book. [2]And many of those who sleep in the dust of the earth shall awake, some to everlasting life, and some to shame and everlasting contempt. [3]And those who are wise shall shine like the brightness of the firmament; and those who turn many to righteousness, like the stars for ever and ever. [4]But you, Daniel, shut up the words, and seal the book, until the time of the end. Many shall run to and fro, and knowledge shall increase." [5]Then I Daniel looked, and behold, two others stood, one on this bank of the stream and one on that bank of the stream. [6]And I said to the man clothed in linen, who was above the waters of the stream, "How long shall it be till the end of these wonders?" [7]The man clothed in linen, who was above the waters of the stream, raised his right hand and his left hand toward heaven; and I heard him swear by him who lives for ever that it would be for a time, two times, and half a time; and that when the shattering of the power of the holy people comes to an end all these things would be accomplished. [8]I heard, but I did not understand. Then I said, "O my lord, what shall be the issue of these things?" [9]He said, "Go your way, Daniel, for the words are shut up and sealed until the time of the end... [12]Blessed is he who waits, and comes to the thousand three hundred and thirty-five days. [13]But go your way till the end; and you shall rest, and shall stand in your allotted place at the end of the days."

2

New Testament Apocalyptic Teaching

Matthew

Now we turn to the New Testament and to Our Lord's eschatological teaching. The following sermon on the Mount of Olives is often called "the Synoptic Apocalypse." We find it in all three synoptic gospels. We shall read St Matthew's account from chapters 24 and 25. The parallel accounts are in Mark 13 and Luke 21. I will not provide any advance indications here, nor for the other passages from the New Testament which we shall read. After these passages, I shall make a few brief comments to conclude this second chapter.

Chapter 24

> [3]As he sat on the Mount of Olives, the disciples came to him privately, saying, "Tell us, when will this be, and what will be the sign of your coming and of the close of the age?" [4]And Jesus answered them, "Take heed that no one leads you astray. [5]For many will come in my name, saying, 'I am the Christ,' and they will lead many astray. [6]And you will hear of wars and rumors of wars; see that you are not alarmed; for this must take place, but the end is not yet. [7]For nation will rise against nation, and kingdom against kingdom, and there will be famines and earthquakes in various places: [8]all this is but the beginning of the birth-pangs. [9]Then they will deliver you up to tribulation, and put you to death; and you will be hated by all nations for my name's sake. [10]And then many will fall away, and betray one another, and hate one another. [11]And many false prophets will arise and

lead many astray. [12]And because wickedness is multiplied, most men's love will grow cold. [13]But he who endures to the end will be saved. [14]And this gospel of the kingdom will be preached throughout the whole world, as a testimony to all nations; and then the end will come. [15]So when you see the desolating sacrilege spoken of by the prophet Daniel, standing in the holy place (let the reader understand), [16]then let those who are in Judea flee to the mountains; [17]let him who is on the housetop not go down to take what is in his house; [18]and let him who is in the field not turn back to take his mantle. [19]And alas for those who are with child and for those who give suck in those days! [20]Pray that your flight may not be in winter or on a sabbath. [21]For then there will be great tribulation, such as has not been from the beginning of the world, until now, no, and never will be. [22]And if those days had not been shortened, no human being would be saved; but for the sake of the elect those days will be shortened. [23]Then if any one says to you, 'Lo, here is the Christ!' or 'There he is!' do not believe it. [24]For false Christs and false prophets will arise and show great signs and wonders, so as to lead astray, if possible, even the elect. [25]Lo, I have told you beforehand. [26]So, if they say to you, 'Lo, he is in the wilderness,' do not go out; if they say, 'Lo, he is in the inner rooms,' do not believe it. [27]For as the lightning comes from the east and shines as far as the west, so will be the coming of the Son of man. [28]Wherever the body is, there the eagles will be gathered together. [29]Immediately after the tribulation of those days the sun will be darkened, and the moon will not give its light, and the stars will fall from heaven, and the powers of the heavens will be shaken; [30]then will appear the sign of the Son of man in heaven, and then all the tribes of the earth will mourn, and they will see the Son of man coming on the clouds of heaven with power and great glory; [31]and he will send out his angels with a loud trumpet call, and they will gather his elect from the four winds, from one end of heaven to the other. [36]But of that day and hour no one knows, not even the angels of heaven, nor the Son, but the Father only. [37]As were the days of Noah, so will be the coming of the Son of man. [38]For as in those days before the flood they were eating and drinking, marrying and giving in marriage, until the day when Noah entered the ark, [39]and they did not know until the flood came and swept them all away, so will be the coming of the Son of man. [40]Then two men will be in the field; one is taken and one is left. [41]Two women will be grinding at the mill; one is taken and one is left. [42]Watch therefore, for you do not know on what day your Lord is coming. [43]But know this, that if the householder had known in what part of the night the thief was coming, he would have watched and would not have let his house be broken into. [44]Therefore you also must be ready; for the Son of man is coming at an hour you do not expect."

Chapter 25

[31]"When the Son of man comes in his glory, and all the angels with him, then he will sit on his glorious throne. [32]Before him will be gathered all the nations, and he will separate them one from another as a shepherd separates the sheep from the goats, [33]and he will place the sheep at his right hand, but the goats at the left... [46]And they will go away into eternal punishment, but the righteous into eternal life."

Now let us turn to some passages from St Paul's Epistles to the Corinthians and Thessalonians.

I Corinthians

Chapter 15

[12]Now if Christ is preached as raised from the dead, how can some of you say that there is no resurrection of the dead? [13]But if there is no resurrection of the dead, then Christ has not been raised; [14]if Christ has not been

raised, then our preaching is in vain and your faith is in
vain. [15]We are even found to be misrepresenting God,
because we testified of God that he raised Christ, whom
he did not raise if it is true that the dead are not raised.
[16]For if the dead are not raised, then Christ has not been
raised. [17]If Christ has not been raised, your faith is futile
and you are still in your sins. [18]Then those also who
have fallen asleep in Christ have perished. [19]If for this
life only we have hoped in Christ, we are of all men most
to be pitied. [20]But in fact Christ has been raised from the
dead, the first fruits of those who have fallen asleep.
[21]For as by a man came death, by a man has come also
the resurrection of the dead. [22]For as in Adam all die, so
also in Christ shall all be made alive. [23]But each in his
own order: Christ the first fruits, then at his coming
those who belong to Christ. [24]Then comes the end, when
he delivers the kingdom of God the Father after destroy-
ing every rule and every authority and power. [25]For he
must reign until he has put all his enemies under his feet.
[26]The last enemy to be destroyed is death. [27]"For God
has put all things in subjection under his feet." But when
it says, "All things are put in subjection under him," it is
plain that he is excepted who put all things under him.
[28]When all things are subjected to him, then the Son himself will also be subjected to him who put all things under him, that God may be everything to everyone...
[35]But some one will ask, "How are the dead raised? With
what kind of body do they come?" [36]You foolish man!
What you sow does not come to life unless it dies. [37]And
what you sow is not the body which is to be, but a bare
kernel, perhaps of wheat or of some other grain. [38]But
God gives it a body as he has chosen, and to each kind of
seed its own body. [39]For not all flesh is alike, but there
is one kind for men, another for animals, another for
birds, and another for fish. [40]There are celestial bodies
and there are terrestrial bodies; but the glory of the celestial is one, and the glory of the terrestrial is another.
[41]There is one glory of the sun, and another glory of the

moon, and another glory of the stars; for star differs from star in glory. [42]So is it with the resurrection of the dead. What is sown is perishable, what is raised is imperishable. [43]It is sown in dishonor, it is raised in glory. It is sown in weakness, it is raised in power. [44]It is sown a physical body, it is raised a spiritual body. If there is a physical body, there is also a spiritual body. [45]Thus it is written, "The first man Adam became a living being"; the last Adam became a life-giving spirit. [46]But it is not the spiritual which is first but the physical, and then the spiritual. [47]The first man was from the earth, a man of dust; the second man is from heaven. [48]As was the man of dust, so are those who are of the dust; and as is the man of heaven, so are those who are of heaven. [49]Just as we have borne the image of the man of dust, we shall also bear the image of the man of heaven. [50]I tell you this, brethren: flesh and blood cannot inherit the kingdom of God, nor does the perishable inherit the imperishable. [51]Lo! I tell you a mystery. We shall not all sleep, but we shall all be changed, [52]in a moment, in the twinkling of an eye, at the last trumpet. For the trumpet will sound, and the dead will be raised imperishable, and we shall be changed. [53]For this perishable nature must put on the imperishable, and this mortal nature must put on immortality. [54]When the perishable puts on the imperishable, and the mortal puts on immortality, then shall come to pass the saying that is written: "Death is swallowed up in victory." [55]"O death, where is thy victory? O death, where is thy sting?" [56]The sting of death is sin, and the power of sin is the law. [57]But thanks be to God, who gives us the victory through our Lord Jesus Christ.

1 Thessalonians

Chapter 4

[13]But we would not have you ignorant, brethren, concerning those who are asleep, that you may not grieve as others do who have no hope. [14]For since we believe that

Jesus died and rose again, even so, through Jesus, God
will bring with him those who have fallen asleep. ¹⁵For
this we declare to you by the word of the Lord, that we
who are alive, who are left until the coming of the Lord,
shall not precede those who have fallen asleep. ¹⁶For
the Lord himself will descend from heaven with a cry of
command, with the archangel's call, and with the sound
of the trumpet of God. And the dead in Christ will rise
first; ¹⁷then we who are alive, who are left, shall be
caught up together with them in the clouds to meet the
Lord in the air; and so we shall always be with the Lord.
¹⁸Therefore comfort one another with these words.

Chapter 5

¹But as to the times and the seasons, brethren, you have
no need to have anything written to you. ²For you yourselves know well that the day of the Lord will come like
a thief in the night. ³When people say, "There is peace
and security," then sudden destruction will come upon
them as travail comes upon a woman with child, and
there will be no escape. ⁴But you are not in darkness,
brethren, for that day to surprise you like a thief. ⁵For
you are all sons of light and sons of the day; we are not of
the night or of darkness. ⁶So then let us not sleep as others do, but let us keep awake and be sober.

2 Thessalonians

Chapter 2

¹Now concerning the coming of our Lord Jesus Christ
and our assembling to meet him, we beg you, brethren,
²not to be quickly shaken in mind or excited, either by
spirit or by word, or by letter purporting to be from us, to
the effect that the day of the Lord has come. ³Let no one
deceive you in any way; for that day will not come, unless the rebellion comes first, and the man of lawlessness
is revealed, the son of perdition, ⁴who opposes and ex-
alts himself against every so-called god or object of wor-

ship, so that he takes his seat in the temple of God, proclaiming himself to be God. [5]Do you not remember that when I was still with you I told you this? [6]And you know what is restraining him now so that he may be revealed in his time. [7]For the mystery of lawlessness is already at work; only he who now restrains it will do so until he is out of the way. [8]And then the lawless one will be revealed, and the Lord Jesus will slay him with the breath of his mouth and destroy him by his appearing and his coming. [9]The coming of the lawless one by the activity of Satan will be with all power and with pretended signs and wonders, [10]and with all wicked deception for those who are to perish, because they refused to love the truth and so be saved. [11]Therefore God sends upon them a strong delusion, to make them believe what is false, [12]so that all may be condemned who did not believe the truth but had pleasure in unrighteousness.

Now we turn to our final scriptural passages for this chapter, from the Epistles of St Peter and St John.

2 Peter

Chapter 3

[1]This is now the second letter that I have written to you, beloved, and in both of them I have aroused your sincere mind by way of reminder; [2]that you should remember the predictions of the holy prophets and the commandment of the Lord and Savior through your apostles. [3]First of all you must understand this, that scoffers will come in the last days with scoffing, following their own passions, [4]and saying, "Where is the promise of his coming? For ever since the fathers fell asleep, all things have continued as they were from the beginning of creation." [5]They deliberately ignore this fact, that by the word of God heavens existed long ago, and an earth formed out of the water and by means of water, [6]through which the world that then existed was deluged with wa-

ter and perished. [7]But by the same word the heavens and
earth that now exist have been stored up for fire, being
kept until the day of judgment and destruction of
ungodly men. [8]But do not ignore this one fact, beloved,
that with the Lord one day is as a thousand years, and a
thousand years as one day. [9]The Lord is not slow about
his promise as some count slowness, but is forbearing toward you, not wishing that any should perish, but that all
should reach repentance. [10]But the day of the Lord will
come like a thief, and then the heavens will pass away
with a loud noise, and the elements will be dissolved with
fire, and the earth and the works that are upon it will be
burned up. [11]Since all these things are thus to be dissolved, what sort of persons ought you to be in lives of holiness and godliness, [12]waiting for and hastening the
coming of the day of God, because of which the heavens
will be kindled and dissolved, and the elements will melt
with fire! [13]But according to his promise we wait for new
heavens and a new earth in which righteousness
dwells. [14]Therefore, beloved, since you wait for these, be
zealous to be found by him without spot or blemish, and at
peace.

1 John

Chapter 2

[18]Children, it is the last hour; and as you have heard that
antichrist is coming, so now many antichrists have
come; therefore we know that it is the last hour. [19]They
went out from us, but they were not of us; for if they had
been of us, they would have continued with us; but they
went out, that it might be plain that they all are not of us.
[20]But you have been anointed by the Holy One, and you
all know. [21]I write to you, not because you do not know
the truth, but because you know it, and know that no lie
is of the truth. [22]Who is the liar but he who denies that
Jesus is the Christ? This is the antichrist, he who denies
the Father and the Son.

Chapter 3

> [2]Beloved, we are God's children now; it does not yet appear
> what we shall be, but we know that when he appears we
> shall be like him, for we shall see him as he is. [3]And every
> one who thus hopes in him purifies himself as he is pure.

You will no doubt have noticed echoes of some of the Old
Testament passages in the New Testament. But this is of less
importance than the details of the eschatological teaching.
You have now read the greater part of the teaching on the end
time to be found in these New Testament readings, other than
that in the Apocalypse (to which we shall turn later). It is extremely important that we bear the whole of this teaching in
mind. It is an essential part of our Orthodox Christian faith, a
part which we are all too often tempted to relegate to a subsidi-
ary position in our thoughts and prayers. Any interpretation of
the Apocalypse must be in accord with what we have read.

In the Synoptic Apocalypse, there is no promise of better
times to come. There are to be no worldly utopias. There will be a
falling away from the faith; love will grow cold. There will also
be many antichrists, those who make false claims to be Christ.
The end time will be one of great tribulation; but, in his mercy,
God will set a limit on this. At the Parousia, the Second Coming,
Christ will appear in power and great glory, and his elect (that is,
those who are his) will be gathered up; others will be left. Only
the Father knows when that day will be: our duty is to watch and
be ready for it. When the day comes, Christ will sit in judgment
on the nations, that is, those who have not been gathered, and
those who have done evil will receive eternal punishment,
whereas the righteous shall join the gathered in receiving eternal
life.

In the passages from the epistles, Our Lord's teaching is reiterated and amplified. St Paul, you must remember, like St
John was caught up and given an apocalyptic revelation, only

part of which he is able to reveal. In writing to the Corinthians, he emphasizes that faith in the resurrection of Jesus Christ and faith in the general resurrection are connected. He stresses that there is an order of resurrection: Christ first, then those who are his at his Second Coming, then the end, that is the general resurrection, the judgment, and the yielding up of the Kingdom by Christ to the Father. This distinction between the resurrection of those who are "in Christ" and the general resurrection is important; the New Testament speaks either of the resurrection "out of" the dead or of the resurrection "of" the dead. St Paul also uses the analogy of the seed to stress that there is continuity as well as glorifying change in the resurrection of the body. And, writing to the Thessalonians, he points to an order of resurrection of the faithful at the Parousia: here, first, the dead in Christ; then, those who remain alive. Note that this eschatological teaching is intended to comfort us, not to fill us with fear! Later, he tells us of the man of lawlessness, full of power and wonders, who must be revealed before the Parousia. St Peter warns us to remember the predictions of the prophets and our Lord's words about the Second Coming, and to beware of those who scoff because everything seems to go on as before. There are many such persons around, including (I fear) some who claim to be Christians. He reminds us that it is the Lord's wish that all should repent and none perish. St John speaks, as does St Paul, of the antichrists, and of the hope that we shall become like the risen Christ. Our task (as St Peter tells us) is to live lives of holiness, and both to await and hasten the day of God. How can we hasten it?—surely only by being servants who are ready, and who pray continually the apocalyptic prayer: "Even so, come, Lord Jesus."

3

Background, History and Structure of the Apocalypse

We have seen that before approaching the Apocalypse, it is important that we have some familiarity with the apocalyptic imagery of the Old Testament: the book of Ezekiel, because it has a structure which the Apocalypse parallels in a remarkable way and because it is full of apocalyptic language, and the book of Daniel because its apocalyptic imagery is so close to that used by St John. It is essential that any interpretation of the Apocalypse should be in accord with the eschatological teaching in the remainder of the New Testament: Our Lord's sermon on the Mount of Olives, the Synoptic Apocalypse, and the teaching of St Paul on the resurrection of the dead, together with passages from the epistles of St Peter and St John. Nowhere do we find any promise of earthly utopias. Quite the reverse is true; faith and love will grow cold, only a remnant of the faithful will remain. There will be wars and great destruction and the appearance of antichrist before the present dispensation ends with the Parousia, the Second Coming of Christ. There is a clear teaching about the order of resurrection: first Christ himself, then, at the Parousia, those who sleep in the Lord, followed by those faithful who are alive at His coming. Finally, there is the general resurrection and judgment of all the nations, and the presentation of the Kingdom of Christ to the Father. All this is manifestly clear from the New Testament teaching.

Another essential prerequisite to any understanding of the Apocalypse is an appreciation of its structure. Without such an appreciation, the book may seem to be somewhat chaotic. This chapter will look at that structure and see what kind of framework can be built up to help us understand its content when we come to the actual text in the remaining chapters. Since virtually every modern commentary on the Apocalypse raises questions of authorship and dating, these matters will be discussed briefly, if only in an attempt to give some support to our own Orthodox tradition that it was written in Patmos by the Evangelist, St John the Apostle, in the latter part of the first century. Some historically significant interpretations will be considered, but first, some general remarks about the book itself and about the nature and purpose of apocalyptic writing are necessary.

Apocalyptic writers appear during times of special affliction. Their purpose is to attack all that weakens or corrupts the people of God and to strengthen the resolve of the faithful enduring persecution; but it is to instill hope rather than fear. Jewish apocalyptic works have a central theme which we can summarize as follows: the world is dominated by a tyrannous evil power, which will continue to inflict sufferings upon the people of God until they rise up under a divinely-sent leader to overthrow it, after which they will inherit the earth and set up a kingdom surpassing all previous kingdoms and with no successor. Christian apocalyptic took over the Jewish symbolism but focused on Christ, with a greater emphasis on a program of events preceding the end. In all apocalyptic writings, persecution will be followed by the vindication of the faithful and the judgment of both the persecutors and the apostates who assist them. This is particularly apparent in both Daniel and the Apocalypse, both of which contain a chronology of eschatological events intended to persuade the reader of the eventual triumph of God and his saints. Daniel was written in the second century BC at the time of the persecutions under Antiochus IV Epiphanes, who, aided and abetted by apostate Jews, was attempting to stamp out Jewish religious observances. The Apocalypse was written following the Roman persecutions and in the period of the enforcement of emperor-worship. Daniel refers back to those Jews who remained faithful during the Babylonian captivity. The Apocalypse relates to the Church, the spiritual Israel, and warns of both a contemporary and a future captivity in the spiritual Babylon, drawing a sharp contrast between the faithful Church and the church contaminated by the world. In both works, contemporary and future events play a part. The word "apocalypse" means "unveiling": apocalyptic writing unveils both the meaning of contemporary events and also a sequence of events to come.

There are, however, important differences between Jewish and Christian apocalyptic writings. In Jewish apocalyptic, the ultimate kingdom to be ushered in by the Messiah is essentially an earthly kingdom, though we can occasionally discern, especially in writings of the inter-testamental period (such as Enoch, the Twelve Patriarchs, Baruch, and Esdras, written at a time of disillusion with the Maccabean kingdom), a tension between the earthly, political, prophetic kingdom and the other-worldly, eternal and universal kingdom of visionaries. It has been suggested that the concept of the Millennium as a temporary messianic earthly kingdom (about which I shall have more to say later) arose as an attempt to bridge the gap. There are also certain significant differences of imagery—the Old Testament lion, for example, becomes the New Testament lamb. Thus, the Old Testament concept of an angry and almost vengeful God is replaced by the Christian revelation of God as the God of love. The expression "the wrath of God" takes on a new meaning in the New Testament, and the appalling judgments which befall sinful man are now seen not in terms of divine vengeance, but as the inevitable consequences which sinful man brings upon himself, permitted by God in the light of man's freedom to accept or reject him. In the Christian Apocalypse, God's strength and ultimate victory lie not in overpowering force, but in self-sacrificing love.

We might also note that Jewish apocalyptic writing was pseudonymous. Because the prophets belonged to what was considered to be a holy period of the past, their number was considered to have been completed. New prophetic writings had little hope of being accepted. Therefore, unless attributed to established figures, as was the case with the book of Daniel, they had no chance of acceptance. The writer of the Apocalypse, however, clearly announces himself as "John," not once but four times.

The theme of the Apocalypse, the great crown and the climax of Holy Scripture, is the certainty of God's ultimate triumph. Its purpose is to attack immorality and idolatry in the Church, and to strengthen faith in the unfailing purposes of God and the final victory of righteousness. It presents the Creator as being also the Redeemer. Nowhere else in the New Testament is the divinity of Christ more comprehensively emphasized. The hope which the apocalyptic expectation of the Second Coming presents was one of the main strengths of the early Church. It was not surprising, therefore, that it is the most quoted work in extant second century Christian writings, and one from which we can learn much, not only of the beliefs but also of the worship of first-century Christians. The certainty with which it proclaims the victory over death did much to encourage the courting of martyrdom.

The Apocalypse is a divinely-inspired meditation on Our Lord's eschatological teaching, expanding in three stages upon the Sermon on the Mount of Olives: the waiting of the saints, the rise of antichrist, and the final triumph over evil. Much of what it treats transcends human understanding. Its language is symbolic, speaking spiritual truths to the spirit of man. It is an impressionist painting in sound, not a series of photographs or press reports, because it tells not merely of the things of earth but also of heavenly activities spilling over into the world. In much of it, time (as we experience it) does not apply. The Alpha is also the Omega, the end is also the beginning; in Heaven past, present and future are as one. And in our Christian experience here on earth, nowhere is this more true than in our participation in the eucharist. Our Orthodox liturgy is an eschatological event. We have the Trisagion, the Cherubic Hymn, the Anaphora (which follows an apocalyptic scheme—we join the archangels, angels, cherubim and seraphim in their triumphant song), the incense symbolizing intercession, and Holy Communion, in which we experience an anticipation of salvation from the last enemy (death) through our participation in the risen life of Christ. In the same way, we find eucharistic references in the Apocalypse, especially in those passages which reflect the worship of the Asian churches and in the great hymns of praise which are scattered throughout the book. This subject will be expanded later.

The symbolic language which we find throughout the Apocalypse is a language of imagery which is entirely Jewish, but it is written in unsophisticated Greek. In this it contrasts with the Greek of the fourth gospel, and this contrast underlies much of the continuing debate about authorship, though the same evidence could also be used to challenge the authorship of the gospel. Yet it is not really surprising that the Greek of the Apocalypse should raise difficulties. Hebrew lacks words representing abstract concepts. As an example, we would say that God is both immanent and transcendent, but the Hebrew Scriptures would and actually do say: "Who is like the Lord our God, who is seated on high, who looks far down upon the heavens and the earth?" (Psalm 112, LXX). Jewish writers had no concept of infinity, nor did the Greeks. This gives rise to considerable difficulties in eschatological writings. Hebrew writers often resorted to pure symbolism, a symbolism which became stylized and hence needed interpretation. Since the Apocalypse is couched in accord with such Hebrew symbolism and contains many quotations from the Psalms and from the prophetic and apocalyptic Old Testament books, and further, since its author may well have been thinking largely in Aramaic, it is not surprising that the Greek differs manifestly from that of the fourth Gospel. Yet we can set against this divergence of language a number of important conceptual convergences as well as some identities of phraseology, especially the way in which the Cross is viewed in terms of judgment. The corresponding passages in the twelfth chapter of the Gospel and the twelfth chapter of the Apocalypse, the centrality of the "Lamb of God" in both works, and the soteriology (the salvation doctrine) of both are all examples of this convergence.

The argument about authorship is not exclusively a modern one, it goes back to Dionysios of Alexandria in the third century, who seems to have been the first to have raised the question. Before this, there is unanimous agreement among the Fathers that the author of the Apocalypse is St John the Theologian, the writer of the fourth Gospel and three epistles. Most of the Fathers after Dionysius would agree with this view. Irenaeus, Hippolytus, Clement, Justin Martyr, Tertullian, Origen, Ephrem the Syrian, Epiphanius, Basil the Great, Hilary, Athanasius, Gregory the Theologian, Ambrose, to mention a few, all accept Johannine authorship. Canon 33 of the Council of Carthage explicitly ascribes the Apocalypse to St John. There is a remarkable convergence of patristic witness to this tradition, a witness which very few Fathers question. Dionysius' arguments, also found in Eusebius, are manifestly exaggerated and even extend to the authorship of the fourth Gospel. This suggests that there was some ulterior motive in his putting them forward. Such a motive is not difficult to find in the case of the Apocalypse. This motive is the heresy of "chiliasm," the belief that, at the Parousia and before the general resurrection and judgment, Christ will establish a kingdom on earth which will last for a thousand years.

Mention of a millennial kingdom in Scripture is confined to the Apocalypse, where it occupies only a few verses in Chapter 20. It can be viewed as a symbolic but natural extension of the days of creation. Acceptance of the idea of millennialism was almost universal in the post-apostolic age. It was taught, for example, by Papias, Justin Martyr, Irenaeus, and many other early Fathers. However, in the second and third centuries, among some heretical sects such as the Montanists, Ebionites and Apollinarians, there arose a literal and highly exaggerated form of millenarian doctrine (associated initially with the name of Cerinthus), which taught that the millennial kingdom would provide extensively for all the fleshly desires. There would be much eating and drinking, and even debauchery and all the lusts would be satisfied. The heaven of Islam is very similar to this description. This teaching spread and the Alexandrians became alarmed at the increasing popularity of this dangerous heresy. The heresy of chiliasm, was eventually condemned in 381 by the Second Ecumenical Council (I Constantinople), which inserted into the Creed the words "Whose kingdom shall have no end" in order to refute the doctrine of a thousand-year kingdom on earth. Later interpreters of the Apocalypse either spiritualized or allegorized the millenial kingdom, though Augustine adopted a historical interpretation, declaring it to be the first thousand years of the Christian Church. This had extraordinary consequences as the year 1000 approached, and there was widespread alarm that the Day of Judgment was drawing near as the first millennium came to a close. Many people in all walks of life gave up their evil habits, clergy abandoned their mistresses, monasteries distributed their wealth to the surrounding poor, bishops threw away their silver and jewelry and sought entrance to the monasteries. Similar events took place around what was considered to be the thousandth anniversary of Pentecost. Such widespread abandoning of sin was not to last; by the middle of the eleventh century things had returned to normal!

Augustine's historical interpretation, which continued to find favor especially in the Roman Church, cannot possibly be the correct one. It is quite clearly stated in the Apocalypse that during the Millennium the devil is bound up, but St Peter in his first Epistle writes: "Your adversary the devil prowls around like a roaring lion, seeking someone to devour." Returning to Dionysius' objections to the Johannine authorship of the Apocalypse, it seems not unlikely that these can be accounted for by his opposition to the teachings of the chiliasts. Most, but not all, modern commentators have adopted Dionysius' arguments, extending them by further detailed examination of the texts. Their arguments are often highly selective and do no more than support plausible hypotheses which are not strong enough to overthrow the Orthodox tradition.

The majority of commentators today follow the lead of Irenaeus and other Fathers in placing the date of composition during the last decade of the the first century, in the reign of Domitian. There are problems with this date and there is a body of opinion supporting a significantly earlier date during the 60s, in the reign of Nero. Supporters of this earlier dating (and the late John Robinson is included among them) have to admit that the external evidence suggests the 90s, but argue that there is internal evidence for the 60s which outweighs it: notably a passage which appears to place the destruction of Jerusalem (AD 70) in the future; another which seems to provide a symbolic list of emperors culminating in Nero; and the intensity of the fulminations against Babylon, thought to be more appropriate to the persecutions under Nero than the calmer times of Domitian. However, this internal evidence has been shown to be highly inconclusive (see, for example, Sweet's commentary mentioned in chapter 1). Passages can be quoted which suggest a date after the eruption of Vesuvius in 79. The intensity of the fulminations against Babylon can relate to past experiences of the writer. They do not have to refer to contemporary events, and any attempt to identify the emperors referred to is hopelessly complicated by the absence of any clear starting-point and the number of pretenders to the imperial throne, some of whom may have to be included in the calculations. It is not certain, either, whether John was referring to emperors or persecutors. We must also remember that, though it is now accepted that the idea of intense persecution under Domition is largely mistaken, it was Domitian who required that he be addressed as "Lord and God"; and this blasphemy may have seemed to the writer of the Apocalypse a worse crime than the earlier persecutions. Arguments against the later dating appear to ignore this.

Attempts to invent hypothetical persons who might have written the Apocalypse do not carry much conviction. The most popular of these is a certain John the Elder (or Presbyter), said to have been (possibly) a disciple of the Apostle John. However, we should note that this is precisely how John announces himself at the beginning of both the second and third Epistles. A highly powerful argument confirming the apostolic authorship of the Apocalypse is the pastoral authority with which it is introduced and concluded. Surely, only an apostle would express such authority to the Seven Churches of Asia.

Some readers may be somewhat bored by such seemingly tortuous academic arguments, but they should be aware of the hypotheses which appear in commentaries and perhaps be reassured by the fact that they do not conclusively overthrow the Orthodox tradition deriving from the early Fathers—namely, that the Apocalypse was written by the Apostle John, author of the Fourth Gospel, on the Isle of Patmos in the last decade of the first century. We can visit the Cave of the Apocalypse (as I have done) without feeling that we are divorcing ourselves from history. In any event, it is the content of the Scriptures which should be our main concern, rather than speculations about authorship which will probably never be settled.

A brief overview of the history of the Apocalypse is necessary now, bearing in mind that its origin has been discussed and its importance noted in the Patristic period, both as a principal source of Christian eschatology and as a stimulus for the chiliast heresy. It was not until the fourth century that the canon of Holy Scripture was finalized. Apostolic authorship was one of the criteria used. Thus the Church formally accepted the traditional view of authorship and rejected the arguments of Dionysius. But there was also a criterion of apostolic content. The Apocalypse would not have been included in the canon if its content had not been considered to be in accord with other apostolic writings. Its inclusion continued to be challenged, however, from time to time, most notably in the East until at least the sixth century. Even as late as the eleventh century, there are doubts expressed as to its appropriateness within the canon of the New Testament.

If eschatology, and the return of Christ in particular, was a significant aspect of early Christian belief, interest in it diminished following the Constantinian settlement of the fourth century. Allegorical and moral interpretations of the Apocalypse became more numerous, and the Parousia was pushed largely out of the mind as belonging to some far future age of history. But in the Middle Ages, the Apocalypse became associated with revolutionary and charismatic groups of oppressed peasantry, particularly in times of war, plague and famine. These people were essentially anarchists, calling for the downfall of both church and state, armed with a literal interpretation of the Apocalypse as their gospel. (It is interesting to note that they were, for the most part, also violently anti-Semitic). In the 12th century, Joachim of Floris, who wrote a commentary on the book, declared that the papal throne would soon be held by antichrist. He also prophesied that the Age of the Spirit was soon to be ushered in by two new orders of monks, and he thus came to be regarded as a great prophet by the more fanatical Franciscans, who, with the Dominicans, came into existence more or less as Joachim had prophesied, although the Age of the Spirit did not appear. Later, the Reformation provided further opportunity for the identification of the papacy with the antichrist, and the Roman Church with Babylon. This crude, popular exposition can be found among certain Protestant sects today. The many tortuous ways in which the number 666 has supposedly been shown to denote one of the popes or the papacy in general can be a matter of some amusement to any serious student of the Bible.

Luther originally rejected the Apocalypse; but later he accepted it, even to the extent of writing a commentary which adopted the Augustinian view, which by this time saw the Millennium as a thing of the past. He took a highly pessimistic view of the future, seeing it as the age of increasing tribulation, to be relieved only by Christ's Second Coming. Calvin's followers, however, were optimists. They saw the Millennium as a time in the future when peace and prosperity would be brought to all the world by the efforts of righteous men. Only after this had been achieved would Christ return to claim his kingdom.

This latter view was to become especially prominent in the West in the 18th century (associated in England particularly

with the name of Daniel Whitby). Traditional millenarian interpreters did, however, appear from time to time. Two of the
most notable in England were Mede and his follower Isaac
Newton, both of whom wrote commentaries in the seventeenth
century. Millenarian interpretations at this time were extremely rare in Protestant Europe, because they had been condemned in the Confessions of the Lutheran and Reformed
Churches. The 18th century was an age of rationalism and general optimism, and the corresponding eschatology in England
rejected any concept of a supernaturally induced Millennium.
The Calvinist view prevailed in both Church and Dissent, and,
as a result, there was a great upsurge of Protestant missionary
societies, designed to spread the gospel to the ends of the earth
and thus establish by man's efforts the hoped-for universal
Christian dispensation.

Meanwhile, Roman Catholic writers, finding themselves
in a position where they had to refute increasingly hostile Protestant identification of the papacy with the antichrist, adopted
a largely futurist view of the Apocalypse. The bulk of it was
seen as relating to times far in the future: antichrist and Babylon, being part of that future, could not therefore possibly be
related to any part of the history of the Roman Church. We
might note, however, that there were one or two Roman scholars who attempted historical interpretations of the prophetic
scriptures, amongst whom was the 17th-century interpreter
Bossuet, who identified the two great evils as the Turkish inva-
sions and the Reformation. Some Roman Catholic writers con-
jured up speculative calculations showing that the number 666
could be interpreted as Martin Luther. However, toward the
end of the 18th century, an extraordinary work by a Spanish
Jesuit (writing under the pseudonym "Ben Ezra") appeared
and rapidly achieved considerable notoriety throughout
Europe. He adopted the usual futurist view of the Jesuits, but

equated Babylon and antichrist with a future apostate Roman priesthood. His work enjoyed wide circulation after being translated into English, but it was very soon placed on the Index of Prohibited Books by the Roman authorities.

Protestant optimism received a severe body-blow with the onset of the French Revolution. This event, soon widely interpreted as the herald of the Last Days, gave rise to a great revival of interest in the prophetic Scriptures, and particularly in the Apocalypse. Prophetic societies were set up and prophetic conferences held with a view to determining from the scriptures which prophecies had already been fulfilled in history and which related to events yet to come. The optimistic view of the eighteenth century was largely swept aside, and subsequent interpretation saw the French Revolution (with its regicide and proclamation of atheism) as the onset of the great tribulation. Ever-increasing anarchy was envisaged, an anarchy which could be relieved only by divine intervention, that is, by the Second Coming of Christ. Often, despite flying in the face of what the Scriptures say, actual dates for the return of Christ were confidently prophesied as a result of studies in the Apocalypse. Adventism of one sort or another became a significant and often strident element within the Protestant community, both in Europe and across the North Atlantic in the United States. Today, most of this furor has again died down. Expectation and hope for the Parousia is largely confined to a few sects (some but by no means all of which are charismatic), who tend to maintain it in its more exaggerated forms.

There was a revival of interest in the Apocalypse in 19th-century Russia, and several commentaries were written, though none has been translated into English. It has been suggested that this revival has been continued in the Catacomb Church, which has seen itself in the image of the woman in the wilderness, but this is virtually impossible to verify, though it seems possible in the light of the circumstances in which that body has had to exist. We Orthodox, if we are faithful to Scripture and Tradition, should not merely value this book as a significant part of our spiritual heritage, but we should also have the Parousia as an essential part of our faith and hope. We should obey Our Lord's command to "watch," and we should live always as if the time of his return were near, even though we cannot possibly know when it will take place.

Space has been devoted to the background and history of the Apocalypse because it is important that we should have some knowledge of the way in which it has been used in the past. Though there are quite a number of commentaries which we can describe as "respectable" (even though we may not agree with all their content), there are also many in the second-hand bookshops which represent what we may, perhaps somewhat unkindly call, "the lunatic fringe."

But it is now time to consider the actual structure of the Apocalypse itself, and see if we can make any sense of it. In this task it is more helpful to have alternatives which can be superimposed on each other as required, in much the same way as we shall find that there are different levels of interpretation of one and the same passage. It will, in fact, be virtually impossible to discuss the structure of the book without some mention of interpretation in the wider sense, though I want to postpone any detailed interpretation to the next two chapters. In any interpretations given here, the general significance of passages will be indicated, not possible references to contemporary first-century history. I shall make no claim, however, to be suggesting *the* interpretation of any particular passage, but only what I see as a reasonable one and, hopefully, one which will stimulate our understanding of the Apocalypse.

As was discussed in chapter 1, we can see the Apocalypse as consisting of a prologue (ch 1), an epilogue (ch 22, 6-end), and four sets of "sevens"—7 letters, 7 seals, 7 trumpets, and 7 bowls—with occasional additional material in between. This is only a very coarse structure for the book, and needs considerable amplification because it might suggest the use of one of two possible approaches, neither of which is correct; namely, that we have either a straight sequence of four sevens; or, alternatively, four views of one and the same set of "sevens." However, the situation is more complicated than this. A considerably modified sequential view is probably the most helpful, provided that we look also for possible interrelations between details of the four "sevens" and appreciate that there are significant scene changes between earth and heaven, and insertions of liturgical hymns of praise and other material. We must have in the back of our minds also that the structure is related both to that of Ezekiel and to that of the Synoptic Apocalypse.

We begin by seeing how this coarse model can be amplified, noting the parallels with Ezekiel and Matthew 24:3-25: 13. Chapter 1, the prologue, divides nicely into two parts: verses 1-11 form an opening address (the prologue proper), and verses 12-20 comprise the vision of the Son of Man (a title which we encounter in Daniel). This vision of Christ parallels the vision of God in Ezekiel 1. Chapters 2 and 3 consist of the letters to the seven churches of the Province of Asia (roughly what we call Asia Minor today), and set the scene on earth where Christ is present in his Church. These two chapters relate to Matthew 24:4-5 and 9-12, and parallel the message to the Jews in Ezekiel 2:24.

The scene now changes to heaven. Chapters 4 to 8:1 contain the seven seals, ending with the opening of the seventh seal and silence in heaven, but subdivision is clearly necessary here. The natural division is after chapter 5—chapters 4 and 5 thus forming the first section. These two chapters tell of the vision of God enthroned, with the twenty-four elders, the seven lamps, the four beasts, and the sealed book which only Christ, the Lamb, is worthy to open. The book, of course, represents the Scriptures, and the vision is intended to be one of assurance, reminding the Church of her call to be risen with Christ and emphasizing the decisive significance of His life, death, and resurrection, the full fruition of which is still to come. The seven seals of the book are opened in the remaining section, that is 6:1 to 8:1, though there is a digression after the sixth unsealing. Chapter 7 introduces the sealing of the 144,000 with a glimpse of the eternal state of the righteous—a note of encouragement! The unsealings refer to judgments, which spill down onto the earth from heaven, giving rise to war, famine, and pestilence. It is here that we encounter the famous four horsemen of the Apocalypse, and we should remind ourselves that four is the number symbolizing the earth. We encounter also the slain saints crying "How long?," and then the great cosmic disasters, followed, after the opening of the seventh seal, by a half-hour of silence. (Related verses in Matthew 24 are 6-8, 13-14, and 19-31, and the parallel in Ezekiel is the judgment on the nations—chs 25-32.)

We now come to the seven trumpets and the three woes, 8:2 to 14:20. We should note that the trumpet vision evolves from the seventh seal, the judgment theme being continued, with particular emphasis here on judgments which follow false worship. It is possible to see these trumpet judgments as being those of the final seal. There is an element of overlap here. The trumpets and woes, as we see, take up seven chapters, which clearly need to be broken down into sections. They include, for example, several interpolations in the sequence of judgments. Again, we have events initiated in heaven which have their consequences on earth. But before the first trumpet sounds, we have the angel with the golden censer, verses 3-5, reminding us of Christ's continuing intercession before the

Father. We can then take as the first main section the remainder of chapter 8 together with all of 9. The sounding of the first six trumpets and the judgments follow, in which we can see something of a parallel with the plagues in Egypt, but perhaps here symbolizing attacks on the Church from paganism and false religions. Note that the fifth and sixth trumpets introduce the first two of the three woes.

We now have two interludes. The first, chapter 10, introduces the angel with the little scroll, which John is required to eat before prophesying, a scroll which was bitter in his belly. We can see this as the record of those whose actions have called down the judgments upon mankind. There are ominous thunderings in the background representing the wrath of the Lamb. Though remember here what I have written about the New Testament understanding of God's wrath. The second interlude, 11:1-13, follows immediately upon the first, and introduces the measuring of the Temple and the prophecy concerning the two witnesses. We return then to the final trumpet and woe taking us to the end of chapter 11.

The remaining part of this section, taking us to the end of chapter 14, all of which can be seen either as a general postscript or as an extension of the period of the seventh trumpet, introduces the woman clothed with the sun (that is, the Church), the war in heaven (due to Satan's hostility to the Messiah) culminating in the casting out of Satan, the war on earth waged against the Church by the two beasts (antichrist and the false prophet), and the number 666, followed by the vision of the Son of Man with the redeemed on Mount Zion, the fall of Babylon, and the gathering of the harvest and the vintage (prelude to the Last Judgment). Note here how the scene changes from time to time from heaven to earth and back again. The seven trumpets develop themes in Matthew 24:14-31 and continue the parallel with the judgment passages in Ezekiel 25-32.

This brings us to the last set of four principal sevens, the seven bowls: 15:1 to 22:5. As with the trumpets, we shall find that we have a long narrative at the end, which can be regarded either as a postscript to the whole or as an extension of the events associated with the final bowl. (It is possible to see the seven bowls as being contained within the seventh seal, because it is one of the four beasts from the seals narrative that presents the bowls to the angels. However, this is to introduce a complication which I do not think is particularly helpful). We can divide the bowls narrative into four parts. First, chapters 15 and 16, the pouring out of the wrath of God in the seven plagues contained in the bowls. Again we are reminded of the plagues of Egypt. At 16:17 we hear the voice crying out "It is done!"—just what has been done is then developed in the second part, which takes us on to 19:5. In this second part we encounter the woman on the scarlet beast, the great harlot, and the seven rulers who support her and whose overthrow by the Lamb is first promised and then described. In contrast with the woman clothed with the sun, who represents the faithful Church, we should see the harlot as representing the apostate church which has committed fornication with the world.

The third part begins at 19:6. First we have the marriage of the Lamb with His bride, the faithful Church—all those who are deemed to be truly "in Christ." Then, there is a final loosening of Satan and the battle with Gog and Magog, their destruction by fire from heaven (that is, by divine intervention), and the final ingathering and judgment. The fourth and last part begins with chapter 21 and takes us to 22:5. We have the vision of the new heaven and earth, the new Jerusalem, the water of life and the tree of life, and the eternal reign of Christ and the saints—a final vision of the inevitable triumph of righteousness, the ultimate reassurance for those struggling now here on earth. (The relevant passages of the Synoptic Apocalypse are Matthew

24:29-31 and 37-40, together with 25:1-13. Parallels in Ezekiel are the description of the messianic kingdom [chs 33-37], the attack of Gog from Magog [chs 38-39], and the vision of final glory [chs 40-48].)

Looking back, it is worth nothing that the destruction passages of chapters 6-20 are bracketed between the vision of God, Creator and Redeemer, who makes all things new, chapters 4 and 5, and 21-22:5. This leaves us with the epilogue, 22:6-end. First, there is the assurance that all that has gone before is "faithful and true." There is the repeated promise of Christ's coming. Blessings are pronounced on the faithful together with dire warnings against adding to or taking away from the content of the prophecy. There is a brief prayer for Christ's return and, finally, the Grace.

I would now like to mention some alternative coarse structures which we can superimpose on the more detailed structures that I have just described, and which may suggest further ideas when we study the Apocalypse. They are offered merely as further food for thought. I shall not discuss them, but leave you to consider them for yourselves.

First, it is possible to see the whole book in terms of three unveilings: The Lord and the Church, the unveilings of God's person; the Lord and the world, the unveiling of God's purpose; and the Lord of all, the unveiling of God's power. Second, it is possible to see the book as including three principal aspects: historical, Christ seen as ruling in his universal Church (1:9-3, 22); prophetic, a prologue, epilogue, and four sets of seven, namely seals, trumpets, bowls, and heads (4:1-19, 21); and last, millennial, the final victory and kingdom (21:1-22, 5). Third, it is possible to see the book in terms of a prologue, an epilogue and seven visions: the first, the seven letters, Christ present in the Church on earth (taking us to the end of ch 3); the second, the seven seals, the Church risen with

Christ in heaven (4-8:1); the third, which includes the first six
trumpets, the judgments which follow false worship (8:2-9);
the fourth, which includes the seventh trumpet, the Church seen
as the Body of Christ, but with Satan at work within it (10-13 in-
clusive); the fifth, including the bowls, the saints with Christ on
Mount Zion and the wrath of God poured out on the apostate
church on earth (14-18); the sixth, the preparation for the new
heaven and earth, the appearance of Christ in glory, and the destruction of antichrist and the false prophet (chapter 19); and, finally, the seventh, the Millennium, destruction of Satan,
universal judgment and the presentation of the kingdom to the
Father (20-22:6). Such a scheme of seven visions is attractive
because of the number seven; and, superimposed on the earlier
one, it can provide an alternative structure, though not one that
greatly enhances our understanding of the book, though it is certainly worth mentioning.

There are two final concepts that must be mentioned, one
relating to the scenes of the visions and the other to the repeated sevens. In connection with the scenes, it is possible to
see in the changing locations in which the visions are set a relationship with the three parts of the Mosaic Tabernacle: the
Outer Court, the Holy Place, and the Most Holy Place. Thus,
anything relating to the earth corresponds to the Outer Court,
the Church's worship on earth corresponding to that of its
Brazen Altar. Heavenly worship, such as we see with the angel of incense in chapter 8, corresponds to the Holy Place
with its Golden Altar. Christ alone being able to open the
seals corresponds to the high priest alone entering the Holy of
Holies, and the Second Coming corresponds to the high
priest coming back from within the veil. This is an interesting
method of approaching the apocalyptic imagery, but it is certainly not evident that this was in the mind of St John at the
time of writing.

Then there is the possible significance of half-weeks, the half of 7 being 3-1/2, the "time, two times and half a time" which we encountered in chapter 7 in Daniel. We find this in the Gospels in the half-week of apparent triumph of evil before the resurrection: Christ seized on Thursday, suffering on Friday, and in the tomb on Saturday until the morning of the resurrection. In the Apocalypse there is a corresponding half-week, of years not days, when antichrist appears to triumph before the Second Coming. In both cases, it is the second half of the week in which evil forces exert their maximum power. Throughout the Apocalypse it is possible to detect that the sevens are divided either four and three, or three and four. The first example: the initial four seals release four horsemen, but there is special emphasis on the last three of the seals. Second, half-way through the trumpets, that is, after 3-1/2 eschatological days, an eagle appears and we have the three woes giving the second half of this eschatological week a sinister emphasis. It has been suggested that this half-week concept is a governing principle of the structure of the Apocalypse, which has been seen in itself to be one great half-week (letters, seals, trumpets, and bowls) embracing weeks, all of which are themselves halved.

There we must leave discussion of the structure of the work and turn to a more detailed examination of its various chapters. In the next chapter we shall look at chapters 1-3, the prologue and the letters to the seven churches. The final chapter will discuss the remaining chapters in overview, choosing passages which seem to be of special interest for one reason or another. "Some Questions for Consideration" are provided in order to direct your thoughts to interesting topics and stimulate you to a more complete study of the text of the Apocalypse than has been possible in this short, introductory work.

4

The Letters to the Seven Churches

As we turn to a closer examination of the text of the Apocalypse, we should try to concentrate upon the broad sweep of the visions rather than getting bogged down in the precise interpretation of minute details, though this is perhaps less applicable to the next chapter than to this one. The interpretation of Scripture is possible at different levels, this is an entirely patristic principle! In the case of the seven letters, for example, their original purpose is clearly to edify certain first-century Christian congregations in the Province of Asia. But accepting this obvious truth should not prevent us from extending their application to the whole Church; after all, seven is the number representing completeness. We are therefore entirely justified in giving the seven churches both a literal and a symbolic meaning, and applying them to the Church Catholic throughout history. After all, St Paul's epistles were written to specific congregations or individuals, but that does not prevent our accepting them as of universal application to the Church. So with the rest of the Apocalypse: we may well accept that there are passages referring to the destruction of the Temple, to emperor-worship, to a hoped-for fall of Rome itself, and so on; but this should not prevent us from seeing its prophecies perhaps partly fulfilled in history up to our own day, nor from accepting the larger part of it as a divinely-inspired eschatological prophecy, at least part of the meaning of which can be grasped by prayerful study.

Scripture has been given to us "for our learning." The Canon of Scripture is an undivided whole; we have no right to

neglect parts of it simply because the symbolism is unfamiliar
to us, or because we are aware that a book has been misused in the
past. Indeed, we can learn from such misuse, not least that it was
often promoted by a confusion of symbolic and literal interpretations. We must always be careful, however, not to adopt interpretations which are in conflict with the rest of Scripture and Holy
Tradition. A warning must be issued against attempts to base predictions about the precise course of the future on the Apocalypse
or on any other of the prophetic scriptures.

Now let us turn to the prologue of Apocalypse, that is, to
chapter 1. The first verse tells us straightaway that the Apocalypse is not "The Revelation of St John the Divine," but "the
revelation of Jesus Christ."

Revelation

Chapter 1

[1]The Revelation of Jesus Christ, which God gave him to
show to his servants what must soon take place; and he
made it known by sending his angel to his servant John,
[2]who bore witness to the word of God and to the testimony of Jesus Christ, even to all that he saw. [3]Blessed is
he who reads aloud the words of this prophecy, and
blessed are those who hear, and who keep what is written
therein; for the time is near.

Notice that we have a revelation originally from the Father
to Our Lord Jesus Christ. The stated chain of communication
is God—Jesus—an angel—John—the churches. It is, however, primarily "the testimony of Jesus Christ." It is also about
"things which must soon take place." We should not stake too
much on the word "soon" applied to the prophecies; it means
only that they will soon begin to be worked out, not that they
will soon be completed. Furthermore (as St Peter tells us),
"with the Lord one day is as a thousand years." Here, as in the

epilogue, we have a blessing pronounced on those who read, hear, and keep its words, the word "keep" implying that the book is not only prophetic but also of moral significance: it implies both meditation and action.

> [4]John to the seven churches that are in Asia: Grace to you and peace from him who is and who was and who is to come, and from the seven spirits who are before his throne, [5]and from Jesus Christ the faithful witness, the first-born of the dead, and the ruler of kings on earth. To him who loves us and has freed us from our sins by his blood [6]and made us a kingdom, priests to his God and Father, to him be glory and dominion for ever and ever. Amen. [7]Behold, he is coming with the clouds, and every eye will see him, every one who pierced him; and all tribes of the earth will wail on account of him. Even so. Amen. [8]"I am the Alpha and the Omega," says the Lord God, who is and who was and who is to come, the Almighty. [9]I John, your brother, who share with you in Jesus the tribulation and the kingdom and the patient endurance, was on the island called Patmos on account of the word of God and the testimony of Jesus. [10]I was in the Spirit on the Lord's day, and I heard behind me a loud voice like a trumpet [11]saying, "Write what you see in a book and send it to the seven churches, to Ephesus and to Smyrna and to Per'gamum and to Thyati'ra and to Sardis, and to Philadelphia and to Laodice'a."

We have already noted the significance of the number seven. The expression "Him who is and who was and who is to come" proclaims two things: first, that God is eternal, reiterated in the alpha-omega concept which we hear four verses later. But it also has trinitarian overtones: the Father declared to Moses "I am He Who is"; the Son "was in the beginning with God"; and the Holy Spirit is He whose coming was promised by Christ to his disciples. That trinitarian declaration is made absolutely explicit by the reference to "Jesus Christ" and to "the seven spirits," an expression which denotes the Holy Spirit in his energies in the world. Note that the kingship of Christ is already proclaimed by virtue of his resurrection from the dead. Note also the liturgical ascription of praise: "to him be glory and dominion for ever and ever." Worship is a constantly recurring theme throughout the whole book. There is then the promise of the Parousia, echoing Daniel 7:13: "Behold, there came with the clouds of heaven one like the Son of Man," and also Our Lord's own words in the synoptic Apocalypse: "They will see the Son of Man coming on the clouds of heaven with power and great glory." This is followed by the affirmation "Even so. Amen." which is repeated in the epilogue. John then tells us that he "was in the Spirit on the Lord's day," assuring us of the supernatural nature of the revelation. "The Lord's Day" here does not necessarily mean Sunday. It is much more likely to be a reference to the eschatological eighth day. He has been caught up into a vision of the eternal realities, which he is required to write down in a book and send to the Seven Churches.

[12]Then I turned to see the voice that was speaking to me, and on turning I saw seven golden lampstands, [13]and in the midst of the lampstands one like a son of man, clothed with a long robe and with a golden girdle round his breast; [14]his head and his hair were white as white wool, white as snow; his eyes were like a flame of fire, [15]his feet were like burnished bronze, refined as in a furnace, and his voice was like the sound of many waters; [16]in his right hand he held seven stars, from his mouth issued a sharp two-edged sword, and his face was like the sun shining in full strength. [17]When I saw him, I fell at his feet as though dead. But he laid his right hand upon me, saying, "Fear not, I am the first and the last, [18]and the living one; I died, and behold I am alive for evermore, and have the keys of Death and Hades. [19]Now write what you see, what is and what is to take place hereafter. [20]As for the mystery of the seven stars which you saw in my right hand, and the seven golden lampstands, the seven

stars are the angels of the seven churches and the seven lampstands are the seven churches.

The figure "in the midst of the lampstands" represents Christ present in his Church. He is clothed in vestments signifying both priesthood and kingship, the ephod of a priest and the golden belt of a king. Notice that He appears both like the Son of Man and like the Ancient of Days, echoes of Daniel. We should interpret this as a reference to the human and divine natures of Christ rather than to the persons of the Son and the Father (as indeed we should interpret the icons in which Christ and the Ancient of Days appear side by side). The reference to burnished bronze and the sound of many waters can be taken as indicating the apostolic basis of the Church and the preaching of the Gospel message. The seven stars are the angels of the churches. The sharp two-edged sword coming from the mouth of Christ represents (as it does in Hebrews and Isaiah) the Scriptures, the word of God, and the description of His countenance echoes the transfiguration on Mount Tabor which John had himself witnessed, and which is specifically related in Orthodox hymnology to the Parousia.

John falls at Christ's feet before the unbearable vision of glory (as seen both in icons of the transfiguration and in those of the Apocalypse on Patmos). But he is reassured: Christ declares himself to be not only "the first and the last" but also, by his resurrection, the conqueror of hell and death. Later in the Apocalypse we shall hear much of the enemies of Christ and his Church, but here in the prologue we are reminded that the victory, even over the last enemy, has already been won. The command to John to write down the things he has seen makes it clear that they relate not only to the present but to the future: the Apocalypse is not merely an epistle to the Church, it is also an eschatological prophecy. But it is to be sent to the "angels" of the churches, represented in the vision by the seven stars in Christ's right hand.

There has been much debate about the meaning of the word "angel" here. Literally it means "messenger." The most satisfactory interpretation is that they are the overseers of the congregations, that is, the bishops, but as seen from above in their spiritual and eschatological aspect. It is the last of the Apostles who is to write to them, and it is now upon them that the ultimate authority to be the proclaimers, the messengers of the Gospel to the world is to rest. Notice that the phrase "the angels of the seven churches" implies a corporate body. Just as at Pentecost the Holy Spirit came upon the Apostles as one body, so the prophetic message of the Apocalypse is communicated not to any chief angel, but to the angels as a corporate body of equals representing on earth the authority of Christ in the Church.

Now we will come to the seven letters themselves. It is obviously not possible in the space available to continue through the whole book verse by verse, but it has been a valuable thing to do so far. It is noteworthy that the seven letters have a common structure. Let us, however, read the first letter completely, so that we can see this structure in a specific example. This is the letter to the angel of the Church at Ephesus.

Chapter 2

[1]"To the angel of the church in Ephesus write: 'The words of him who holds the seven stars in his right hand, who walks among the seven golden lampstands. [2]I know your works, your toil and your patient endurance, and how you cannot bear evil men but have tested those who call themselves apostles but are not, and found them to be false; [3]I know you are enduring patiently and bearing up for my name's sake, and you have not grown weary. [4]But I have this against you, that you have abandoned the love you had at first. [5]Remember then from what you have fallen, repent and do the works you did at first. If not, I will come to you and remove your lampstand

from its place, unless you repent. [6]Yet this you have, you hate the works of the Nicola'itans, which I also hate. [7]He who has an ear, let him hear what the Spirit says to the churches. To him who conquers I will grant to eat of the tree of life, which is in the paradise of God.

First, in the letter there is a reference to one of the aspects of Christ as seen in the initial vision. Here He is declared to be the one holding the stars and walking among the lampstands. Next, there is a diagnosis of the state of the particular congregation, for which the angel is responsible as Christ's representative, introduced by the words "I know your works." This diagnosis includes things to be commended (hard work without fainting, patience, hatred of evil, especially the deeds of the Nicolaitans, and discernment of false apostles), but also things deserving censure and their consequences (this church had fallen from its first love and good works, and needed to repent if its lampstand was not to be removed). All this is followed by a command to hear the message and, finally, a promise of reward to "him who conquers." There are thus five main sections after the addressee is named: a reference to Christ; a diagnosis (introduced by "I know your works" and beginning with whatever is deserving of commendation); an exhortation, that is to say, a command with the consequences spelled out if it is not heeded; a call to hear, that is, a demand for spiritual understanding; and a promise to the faithful. The call to hear and the promise are interchanged in the last four letters.

Ephesus was at that time the greatest city of the Asian Province, though both Smyrna and Pergamum (or Pergamos, as the Authorized Version has it) challenged it for primacy. On the shore of the Aegean, Ephesus was a natural starting point for a tour of the province taking in all seven churches, and it was the nearest of the cities to Patmos. According to tradition, John himself lived there for a time and eventually died there. It

was a center of the worship of the goddess Diana and also of
the emperor-cult, both of which had been resisted by the Christians there. There was a significant Jewish community, and
much practice of the magical arts. The Christian church there
was noted for certain deviations from the faith, falling from its
first love and first works (see Acts 20 and 1 Timothy 1). But
the condemnation in the letter may refer to an attitude of un-
loving censoriousness on the part of the more orthodox. Certainly, the signs of apostasy and lack of love, a major theme of
the Apocalypse, were already apparent. The Nicolaitans, followers of an apostate deacon (Nicholas of Antioch), were a
gnostic sect noted for their immorality. The command to hear
refers, of course, to the spiritual ear. It is a call to spiritual discernment which we find in several places in the Gospels. The
promise of the tree of life to "him who conquers" is a reference
to Genesis and the fall of Adam. The curse of Genesis 3 has already been removed in Christ, the New Adam, who has re-
opened the way to paradise and can promise eternal life to
those who overcome evil by living in him. We may note that
the threat to remove the lampstand was eventually carried out.
Although the Third Ecumenical Council was held at Ephesus,
the great and proud city was to become nothing more than a
Moslem village.

The second letter is to the angel of the Church at Smyrna
(2:8-11). Smyrna was a city of great wealth. The church there,
which according to tradition had been founded by St John,
was, however, poor by worldly standards, though rich in the
things of the spirit. Christ is described in the opening passage
as "the first and the last, who died and came to life." Again we
have the alpha and omega theme of the first chapter, together
with a reminder of the resurrection. The Church in Smyrna is
one of the two churches which are exclusively commended,
the other being Philadelphia. It is said, however, to be in immi-

nent danger of persecution by the Romans inspired by the fanatical Jews, called here "a synagogue of Satan." Indeed, they
are described as blasphemers "who say that they are Jews," a
parallel with the false apostles in Ephesus. These were the people who were to take part in the martyrdom of Polycarp around
the middle of the next century. It is declared that some members of the church will be imprisoned through the machina-
tions of the devil, the false accuser; but all this was to be for a
limited period. Those who remained "faithful unto death" are
promised "the crown of life"; and "He who conquers" is as-
sured of escape from "the second death." Reference to "the
crown" was particularly appropriate because Smyrna was famous for its athletic games, echoes here of James 1 and of St
Paul writing to Timothy of "the crown of righteousness." The
"second death" is encountered later in the Apocalypse in
chapters 20 and 21. It refers to the final sentence of the wicked
at the Last Judgment. Smyrna is the last of the seven cities to
experience the eclipse of Christian worship.

The third letter is to the angel at Pergamum. Pergamum was
the old Greek capital, and had become the first center of the
emperor-cult. Both politically and spiritually, therefore, it was
truly "where Satan's throne is." Christ is described as "him who
has the sharp two-edged sword," a reference to 1:16 and referring
to the Scriptures as the word of God which reveals hidden evil.
Loyalty to Christ was dangerous in this city, and one member of
the church, Antipas, had already been martyred. As this would
seem to refer to the bishop, a disciple of John, who was martyred
in AD 92, it is internal evidence for the later dating of the Apocalypse. Christians here are commended for their faithfulness, but
not all! Some have joined the Nicolaitans. The reference to
Balaam is especially important. As we learn from the Book of
Numbers (chs 22-25 and 31), Balak, King of Moab, attempted to
hire him to curse the invading Israelites. Later, it was at

Balaam's instigation that the Children of Israel committed both actual and spiritual fornication with the Moabites, that is, they played "the harlot with the daughters of Moab" and worshiped their gods. Balaam was, therefore, a symbol of those who promoted infidelity. In both Jewish and Christian writings, "fornication" means religious infidelity, and, specifically, contamination through involvement with the world. This theme of harlotry assumes great importance in the prophecies of the Apocalypse, always referring to the apostasy of those who claim to belong to the Church. Apostate Christians are called to repent lest Christ should come and smite them with his mouth, a reference to Isaiah 11:4: "He shall smite the earth with the rod of his mouth, and with the breath of his lips he shall slay the wicked." Again there is the call to hear, followed by a promise to the faithful Christians, this time to be given "hidden manna" and a white stone with "a new name written on the stone, which no one knows except him who receives it." The hidden manna is that which has been kept in the Ark of the Covenant and hidden by Jeremiah before the destruction of the first Temple. Almost certainly, this is a reference to the Eucharist, as it is explicitly in John's gospel (6:31-35). The white stone represents the reward of victory through steadfastness in the faith. Roman judges collected votes by means of black and white stones, black representing "guilty" and white "not guilty." The new name, promised again to the faithful Christian at Philadelphia, represents recognition of change through life in Christ. There may be a reference here to baptism, but it seems unlikely because the name is secret. The knowing of someone's name could signify having power over them, as we see, for example, in the story of wrestling Jacob in Genesis 32. The secrecy of this promised new name is a guarantee of invulnerability, even in the very presence of the throne of Satan, though it also clearly has eschatological significance.

The fourth letter is to the angel at Thyateira, the least important of the seven cities, though this is the second longest of the letters, running to twelve verses (2:18-29). Here Christ is described as the one with "eyes like a flame of fire" and with feet like "burnished bronze," a reference back to 1:14-15. There is commendation for charity, service, faith (that is, faithfulness rather than belief), and patience. However, a woman, Jezebel, a self-proclaimed prophetess, whose name recalls the wife of Ahab who caused Naboth to be put to death (1 Kings 21), has been permitted to teach in the church, corrupting the hearts of the people and seducing them "to practice immorality and to eat food sacrificed to idols." This last was a practical problem which had also faced St Paul (see 1 Corinthians 8). Food sold in the market places had often been part of an offering to idols. Christians were prohibited from knowingly eating such food. Here, however, it also has a symbolic significance, as it is linked with the idea of fornication. There were clearly followers of Jezebel who had compromised themselves with the world. Eating things sacrificed to idols signifies accepting the standards of the world instead of those of the Gospel. Time had been allowed for this false prophetess to repent and for the church to disown her, but she had continued to be accepted as a teacher. Therefore, she would be cast into a sick-bed, and all her children who committed adultery with her (that is, followed her teaching) would be struck dead (that is, would die spiritually, a reference to the Last Judgment) unless they repented. This promise of judgment is a reminder to "all the churches" that Christ will search all hearts, and that all will be judged according to that searching. Those who had remained faithful would have no burden placed upon them other than that already placed on them—presumably this is a reference to the apostolic injunction in Acts 15: "It has seemed good to the Holy Spirit and to us to lay upon you no greater burden than these necessary things: that you abstain from what has been sacrificed to idols and from blood and from what is strangled and from unchastity." Reference to "the deep things of Satan," from which the faithful had preserved themselves, indicates that sorcery was practiced in the city, and emphasizes that Christians must not participate in any form of magical practice. There is a reversal of order at the end of this letter. The command to hear comes at the end, after the promise to the faithful. This time the promise is "power over the nations" and the gift of the morning star. Here, moral power rather than physical power is to be understood. The faithful Christian exercises moral power, not by compromise with the world, but by love and self-sacrifice. This is the secret of Christ's power and authority, and it is an important theme in the Apocalypse. Loving self-sacrifice is a rod of iron which breaks evil into pieces just as a potter's vessel can be broken in pieces by a material iron rod. The "morning star" is, of course, Christ himself, whose life, and hence power, will be given to the faithful, possibly again a eucharistic reference. The idea of Christ as the morning star, which we find again in the epilogue, is a reference to Numbers 24: "A star shall come forth out of Jacob, and a scepter shall rise out of Israel; it shall crush the forehead of Moab, and break down all the sons of Sheth." It is mentioned also in 2 Peter 1:19, where the apostle refers explicitly to the star rising in men's hearts.

We come now to chapter 3 and the last three letters, the first to the angel at Sardis, the ancient capital of the Lydian kingdom of Croesus. But its power lay in the past. Though it was apparently an impregnable fortress, it had twice been captured in night attacks. The theme of the letter is therefore, most appropriately, wakefulness. Christ is here described as the one who has the seven spirits and the seven stars. This church is condemned for having become "dead." It is one of the two churches which receive no commendation. It was once alive, and there are perhaps still possibilities of a return to life to be found in it, since it is called to "strengthen what remains," to remember what it has received, to hold fast to these, and to repent. Even for a church which to all intents and purposes is dead through conformity with the world, there is the possibility of repentance. But Christ will come upon it unexpectedly "like a thief," as promised also in the Synoptic Apocalypse, and the few individuals "who have not soiled their garments" will walk with him in white. Again, in this letter, the final words are the call to hear, preceded by the promise to those who overcome. The promise to the few who remain faithful within this dead church is in two parts. They will be clothed "in white garments," they will be amongst those, seen later in John's vision, who have "washed their robes...in the blood of the Lamb" (7:14). Unlike those who are spiritually dead, they will not have their names blotted "out of the book of life." Notice that this second part of the promise is stated negatively rather than positively. What stands out above all else in the Sardis church is that it has become spiritually dead. This dead majority will not escape the second death.

Philadelphia is the second of the two churches which are exclusively commended, and indeed there are several points which this letter has in common with that to the Church in Smyrna. Philadelphia was a city that had been founded in the second century BC in order to promote Hellenism in Lydia and Phrygia, and so had the character of a missionary city, a point which is echoed in one passage of the letter. But it was subject to earthquakes, again a point which St John picks up. First, Christ is described as "the holy one, the true one, who has the key of David, who opens and no one shall shut; who shuts and no one opens." Here, as with the letter to Smyrna, Christ's titles look back to 1:18. The specific reference to the key of

David and the subsequent passage also echo Isaiah 22, where Eliakim replaces the wicked Sheba as royal steward and is given "the key of the house of David...; so he shall open and none shall shut; and he shall shut and none shall open." Christ is the true steward of the household of God. He alone has the keys of the kingdom, just as, later, it is He alone that can open the sealed scroll. For the Church at Philadelphia the door is declared to be open, for it has kept Christ's word and has not denied his name. This reference to Christ as the door is repeated in Ignatius' letter to the Philadelphians, written at more or less the same time as the Apocalypse. As does Smyrna, the city contains apostate Jews ("the synagogue of Satan"), but here it is declared, "I will make them come and bow down before your feet, and learn that I have loved you." Thus the witness of the church at Philadelphia is to be a successful missionary witness. There now comes the assurance that, because of this faithful witness, this church will be kept "from the hour of trial," and it is called to remain steadfast so that "no one may seize your crown." That crown of life is also promised to the church at Smyrna. The "hour of trial" from which the Philadelphian Christians are promised escape is to become, later in the Apocalypse, the period of great disasters and of the rise of antichrist, a period in which even the elect can be deceived. Rightly do we pray "Lead us not into temptation"! The promise to those who overcome is that they will become pillars in God's temple and will "go no more out." In God's temple there are no earthquakes. They will also be members of the City of God, the New Jerusalem, having its name, together with God's name, written upon them. They will also receive a new name given to them by Christ. Here we have the promise of three names. The first is a reference to Isaiah 62 where we find the promise that Jerusalem shall be "called by a new name," a name which means "sought after." "The name of my God" may well be a reference to baptism. The "new name" given them by Christ parallels the secret name promised to the faithful of Pergamum. The letter ends with the command to "hear."

We come now to the final and longest letter, that to the angel at Laodicea. Laodicea was an important center of commerce as it lay on one of the great trade routes. It was famous for its black wool. There was, however, a curious situation with its water supply. The water originated in hot springs but arrived in the city lukewarm; this is reflected in the diagnosis passage. In AD 61 it suffered earthquake damage, but it was too proud to accept assistance from the imperial court. Many of its citizens, including those of the Christian community, were extremely wealthy and concerned primarily with their business affairs. It is perhaps not surprising that this church receives only condemnation. Here Christ is described as: "the Amen, the faithful and true witness, the beginning of God's creation," the alpha and omega theme again, but with the "Amen" signifying that he is the answer to all the promises of God. The diagnosis of the state of the church and its rejection by Christ is stated unequivocally: "because you are lukewarm, and neither cold nor hot, I will spew you out of my mouth." Christians who have once been hot (fervent in faith) but who have grown lukewarm are worse than those who are cold, never having received the warmth of the faith. The Christians of Laodicea were also puffed up with pride, saying: "I am rich, I have prospered, I need nothing," but they are told that spiritually they are in fact wretched, miserable, poor, blind, and naked; and they are instructed to buy "gold refined in the fire...and white garments" and to anoint their eyes with eyesalve so that they may see. Why "gold"? (here the meaning of course is "spiritual gold"), surely because Christ had himself described "the kingdom of heaven" as "treasure" (see Matthew 13:44). We find this reference to gold again, late in the Apocalypse, when it is said to be the material of the New Jerusalem. And why "buy"? In the same parable in Matthew we are told that its acquisition required that the man should, with joy, first sell all that he had in order to purchase it. This is precisely what Christ had told the rich young man inquiring about the acquisition of eternal life. The "white garments" symbolizes spiritual clothing, in contrast to the black wool, a symbol of commercial wealth. They need eyesalve so that their spiritual eyes might be opened, perhaps a reference to the miracle at the Pool of Siloam where Christ had anointed the blind man's eyes with clay. Again, there is the call to repentance, followed by that wonderful verse that inspired the Holman Hunt picture which hangs in Keble College Chapel, Oxford: "Behold, I stand at the door, and knock; if any one hears my voice, and opens the door, I will come in to him, and eat with him, and he with me." Even though He comes as the master of the house, the door must be opened from the inside. Here we are reminded of the Orthodox concept of "synergy"—God does not impose salvation upon us; it is offered but demands our response. In the same way, it was necessary for Mary to respond, "Be it unto me according to thy word," before she could become the *Theotokos* (the one who gives birth to God). The final promise to those who overcome is to share the throne which is Christ's because he first has conquered. The chapter concludes: "He who has an ear, let him hear what the Spirit says to the churches."

There are many parallels, even repetitions, in the letters. It has been pointed out that, in many ways, the last three mirror the first three. Thus we can see the forces of evil which surround all the churches, including those exclusively commended, characterized as being of four kinds, all of which appear in the first four letters. They are: false apostles; false synagogues; false prophets and godless kings; and royal harlots. These evils are encountered again later in the book, and so I shall be referring back to them in the next chapter. The principal ways in which these evils are seen to have influence within the churches is corruption through contamination with the world, through spiritual adultery with the things of the world.

While virtually all commentators accept that these letters to the seven churches are of general relevance to the Church as a whole in every period of its history, by no means do all accept the idea of a specific chronological application which seeks to suggest that each letter in turn applies to an identifiable period of the Church from the apostolic age to the Parousia. Indeed, some serious commentators would wish specifically to reject such an interpretation. Nevertheless, a sufficient number of commentators, especially since the revival of interest in the prophetic scriptures in Europe in the early 19th century, have done precisely this. We should be aware of the method by which this is done but note that this develops only very late, and in the context of the history of the Church in the West.

The church at Ephesus has been seen as symbolic of the main period of the apostolic age, perhaps up to 60 AD or a little later. Even then, as the New Testament tells us, there were signs of dissention within the Church and of a falling away from the faith. The name "Ephesus" means "desirable," appropriate for the Christian Church faithful to apostolic faith and order.

The church of Smyrna has been seen as symbolic of the period from the onset of the great persecutions under Nero up to the early fourth century, the time of Constantine the Great. It is a period notable for Christian martyrdom and for spiritual growth within the Church, not least the flowering of the desert fathers. "Smyrna" signifies "myrrh," the symbol of suffering and death, so appropriate for the times of the great martyrs.

The church at Pergamum has been associated with the fourth century, the century of the Constantinian settlement when great numbers entered the Church for worldly reasons. It was a period of apparent Christian triumph, but this triumph brought with it the grave dangers of worldly power and ambitions. "Pergamum" signifies "exaltation"; this period is therefore one in which hatred of worldly things has changed for the seeking of worldly approbation.

The church of Thyateira has been said to represent the period of the growth and triumph of the Papacy, and the concept that one man can rule the Church and speak authoritatively on behalf of it. This is interpreted as one form of usurpation of the rule of Christ, who alone is head of the Church. Thyateira signifies "toil," but it is with the toiling of Jezebel within the Church that this idea is seen as being most appropriately associated. The period of Thyateira, therefore, includes the corruption of the faith enshrined in the Creed through medieval doctrinal inventions (such as the doctrines of purgatory and indulgences) and the harnessing of civil power to enforce ecclesiastical discipline, as in the Inquisition. It takes us up, therefore, to the time of the Reformation.

The church at Sardis is the period of ecclesiastical anarchy, leading inevitably to a corresponding time of political anarchy and the overthrow of anointed rulers by atheistic mobs, of which the French and Russian Revolutions are, perhaps, two of the most notable examples. "Sardis" means "that which remains," said to represent here the reduction of the Church to a state of almost complete spiritual poverty. If the period of Thyateira is the period when Christ's rule is usurped by one man, the period of Sardis is that in which Christ's rule is usurped by everyone's individual opinion, and there is a general rejection of the authority of the apostolic tradition of the Church.

This brings us to the present century and beyond, a period in which both Philadelphia and Laodicea can be seen as the types. "Philadelphia" means "love of the brethren" and "Laodicea" signifies "worldly values." In our present age, therefore, we have a specific representation of the wheat and the tares growing together and awaiting the harvest. The church at Philadelphia represents therefore that part of the Church in these latter days (wherever it may be found, and God is the judge of this!) which remains faithful to Holy Tradition, waiting for the promised return of the Lord. This is the faithful remnant spoken of by Isaiah (whom St Paul quotes when writing to the Romans: "a remnant shall be saved"). The church of Laodicea, by contrast, represents that part of the church of the latter days (and Scripture would seem to suggest that this will comprise the majority of those who claim to be Christian) which is so contaminated with the ideas and objectives of the world as to deserve the total rejection declared in the words: "I will spew you out of my mouth." Ultimately, in the final spiritual struggle between the faithful Church (with its eyes set upon heaven) and the false church (with its eyes set upon earth), it is to be a matter of the answer to the ancient question posed by Moses: "Who is on the Lord's side?" This is a matter in which there is no middle way, one in which lukewarmness can have no place. But, until the Parousia, there is always time to change sides, to repent.

Now it is true that there is a kind of seductive appropriateness in much of this sort of chronological analogy between the seven letters and the Church's history, though it should be treated with some caution. Nevertheless, there may be something that we can learn from such an exercise, especially in relation to the days in which we are now living. The contamination of the church by the world is all too apparent! But we need to be on our guard against too naive and literal an extension of the letters to history. In particular, there is the danger of passing judgments which are reserved for God alone, whether they be judgments on the present or on the past. The apparent restriction to Western Christianity in the later periods is also highly dangerous for us Orthodox. Let us not imagine for a moment that we are exempt from the strictures of the letters. We should note especially that the letters were addressed to the churches, so that what they contain is relevant not only to our own personal self-examination as individuals, but also to a self-examination needed in terms of communities and parishes, and jurisdictions. This does not mean that we should try to make specific identifications with the particular churches to which the letters were addressed, but rather that we should measure ourselves, both as individuals and as communities, against all those things singled out for condemnation. We can summarize them as follows: failing to live up to the promises of baptism in faith and works; becoming primarily consumers of the things of this world; corrupting the church and the faith with secular ideas; seeking worldly instead of heavenly objectives; tolerating the presence of false prophets, or even following them; failing to watch for the Lord's coming; having pride in worldly things and achievements; allowing our faith and our love to become lukewarm. Let us not delude ourselves by thinking that our Orthodox churches are not guilty of any of these things. But, remember that the overall message of the Apocalypse is also reflected in these seven letters. The message is that the victory has already been won, that Christ is enthroned on high, and that a share in that throne is offered to all who turn away from the world, repent, set their hearts on the things that are above, and live in him.

5

The Time of the End

We now come to the final chapter and we will spend more time reading the Apocalypse than we have in the earlier chapters. I have chosen passages where I think there are interesting matters of interpretation and which will, taken overall, give a better feel for the work as a whole. We shall first read a passage and then comment on it.

We should try to concentrate here on the broad sweep of images and their significance to avoid getting bogged down in intricate details. We should remember too that the Apocalypse is a mysterious and visionary book. We cannot expect to understand the significance of every word. Most important, it is a book which must speak spiritual messages to our hearts. We are to hear "what the Spirit says." So, we must be careful not to reduce our study merely to an intellectual exercise.

Let us turn first to the scene as it opens in heaven, where John sees the throne of God and the four beasts "in the midst." The chapter opens with the words "After this," signifying the beginning of a new vision, not that we have moved from the past or present into the future.

Revelation

Chapter 4

[1]After this I looked, and lo, in heaven an open door! And the first voice, which I had heard speaking to me like a trumpet, said, "Come up hither, and I will show you what

must take place after this." [2]At once I was in the Spirit, and lo, a throne stood in heaven, with one seated on the throne! [3]And he who sat there appeared like jasper and carnelian, and round the throne was a rainbow that looked like an emerald. [4]Round the throne were twenty-four thrones, and seated on the thrones were twenty-four elders, clad in white garments, with golden crowns on their heads. [5]From the throne issue flashes of lightning and and voices and peals of thunder, and before the throne burn seven torches of fire, which are the seven spirits of God; [6]and before the throne there is as it were a sea of glass, like crystal. And round the throne, on each of the throne, are four living creatures full of eyes in front and behind: [7]the first living creature like a lion, the second living creature like an ox, the third living creature with the face of a man, and the fourth living creature like a flying eagle. [8]And the four living creatures, each of them with six wings, are full of eyes all around and within, and day and night they never cease to sing, "Holy, holy, holy, is the Lord God Almighty, who was and is and is to come!" [9]And whenever the living creatures give glory and honor and thanks to him who is seated on the throne, who lives for ever and ever, [10]the twenty-four elders fall down before him who is seated on the throne and worship him who lives for ever and ever; they cast their crowns before the throne, singing, [11]"Worthy art thou, our Lord and God, to receive glory and honor and power, for thou didst create all things, and by thy will they existed and were created."

The first thing John sees is a door, an echo of the final promise in the letter to the angel at Laodicea. But notice that there is a significant difference: here, Christ does not knock at the door of the human heart and wait for it to be opened; rather, he has himself opened the door into the heavenly places, taking us back to the letter to Philadelphia: "I have set before you an open door." John is summoned by a trumpet-voice, as Moses had been; and the first thing that he sees is a throne and one "seated on the throne." Although there is a symbolic description of the one on the throne in terms later to be applied to the heavenly city, the New Jerusalem, concentration is on the scene in its vicinity, and not on its occupant. We may note here that the colors of the rainbow and the stones, green and fiery-yellow, signify the mercy and the justice of God. The rainbow is a clear reference to God's promise after the flood; but note its color, green for mercy. We are then told of the 24 elders, the seven torches, and the four living creatures. Why are there "twenty-four elders"? This is probably a reference to the 24 heads of priesthood, recorded in 1 Chronicles 24, who had a duty to declare the law, though it may also refer to the 12 Patriarchs and 12 Apostles. One interpretation does not exclude the other, a point that we need continually to bear in mind. The lightning and thundering inform us that this is a throne of judgment. The whole scene is reminiscent of Daniel 7, where we have the enthroned "Ancient of Days," the seated court, together with the books ready to be opened. It is the setting of the scene of the Last Judgment.

We are told that the seven lamps are "the seven spirits of God," the Holy Spirit in his energies (as we have already noted). Here again we have a trinitarian reference similar to that in chapter 1: the Father on the throne, the Son who has opened the door, and the Holy Spirit beside the throne. Later, we shall see the crucified and resurrected Lamb upon the throne, a clear proclamation of the divinity of Christ. Christ and the Father are one. But, as it is the crucified and resurrected Lamb that occupies the Father's throne, Christ is presented also in his humanity.

The "sea of glass, like crystal" is not the storm-tossed sea out of which one of the beasts arises, but the water of purity upon which we later see the saints standing, possibly a baptismal reference.

The four "living creatures," the lion, the ox, the man, and the eagle, each with six wings and full of eyes, are the cherubim. It is a combination of Ezekiel's vision of the four living creatures and Isaiah's vision of the six-winged seraphim. Thus we have the throne, upheld by four cherubim, each with six wings, 24 wings in all, surrounded by the 24 thrones of the elders. But there is a significant change of order. In Ezekiel, the order is: man, lion, ox, eagle. Traditionally these have been associated with the four evangelists, though in Jewish symbolism they represented the four corners of the earth. Here, they may also symbolize the whole economy of Christ: lion, victory over death and hence kingship; ox, the offering of sacrifice, hence high priesthood; man, incarnation; eagle, the giving of the life-creating Spirit. Some commentators have associated them with the signs of the Zodiac, but this interpretation is not helpful. The important thing is that St John puts the lion first. In the unsealings which are to follow, Christ is revealed as the victorious Lion of Judah. Why "full of eyes?" In the next chapter, eyes are specifically related to the Spirit, the one who discerns all things; those who sing the thrice-holy are filled with the Spirit of God.

Chapter 4 ends with the first of the great heavenly hymns of praise. There is surely a liturgical reference here. Notice the antiphonal nature of the singing. First the four living creatures sing a thrice-holy, then the 24 elders sing a response declaring that Christ is worthy to "receive glory and honour and power." This antiphonal presentation is typical of the heavenly hymns of the Apocalypse. Notice also that in this great hymn we have both the trinitarian theme repeated and also the specific identification of Christ as creator. Some commentators have seen this hymn as reflecting the Jewish morning liturgy celebrating creation.

Let us now read chapter 5, where we move from the idea of creation to that of redemption in the same way as the Jewish morning rite of praise was followed by thanksgiving for deliverance at the Red Sea.

Chapter 5

¹And I saw in the right hand of him who was seated on the throne a scroll written within and on the back, sealed with seven seals; ²and I saw a strong angel proclaiming with a loud voice, "Who is worthy to open the scroll and break its seals?" ³And no one in heaven or on earth or under the earth was able to open the scroll or to look into it, ⁴and I wept much that no one was found worthy to open the scroll or look into it. ⁵Then one of the elders said to me, "Weep not; lo, the Lion of the tribe of Judah, the Root of David, has conquered, so that he can open the scroll and its seven seals." ⁶And between the throne and the four living creatures and among the elders, I saw a Lamb standing, as though it had been slain, with seven horns and with seven eyes, which are the seven spirits of God sent out into all the earth; ⁷and he went and took the scroll from the right hand of him who was seated on the throne. ⁸And when he had taken the scroll, the four living creatures and the twenty-four elders fell down before the Lamb, each holding a harp, and with golden bowls full of incense, which are the prayers of the saints; ⁹and they sang a new song, saying, "Worthy art thou to take the scroll and to open its seals, for thou wast slain and by thy blood didst ransom men for God from every tribe and tongue and people and nation, ¹⁰and hast made them a kingdom and priests to our God, and they shall reign on earth." ¹¹Then I looked, and I heard around the throne and the living creatures and the elders the voice of many angels, numbering myriads of myriads and thousands of thousands, ¹²saying with a loud voice, "Worthy is the Lamb who was slain, to receive power and wealth and wisdom and might and honor and glory and blessing!" ¹³And I heard every creature in heaven and on earth and under the earth and in the sea, and all therein, saying, "To him who sits upon the throne and to the Lamb be

blessing and honor and glory and might for ever and ever!" [14]And the four living creatures said, "Amen!" and the elders fell down and worshiped.

The scroll "sealed with seven seals" takes us straight back to Ezekiel 2. It is written both on the inside and the outside, as were the deeds of sale throughout the ancient world; opening it would give effect to its contents (rather like the opening of a will). The proclamation, "Who is worthy to open the scroll?" reminds us of similar occasions in Daniel. The answer here is that no one can open it except the Lion of Judah, David's heir, the Root of Jesse, a reference to Jacob's blessing in Genesis 49, and to the prophecy in Isaiah 11 where the sevenfold gifts of the Spirit are listed. Thus we may see the book as a symbol of the Scriptures, whose meaning is hidden from us until He, who is the subject of the book, opens our eyes through his Spirit. We then see the "Lamb, standing as though it had been slain," indicating to us how the Lion's victory has been won. Victory is achieved through self-sacrificing love. This sudden appearance of the Lamb reminds us of the sudden appearance of the ram which saved Isaac. But we do not see it slain. Christ's sacrifice is once and for all and cannot be repeated. This is an important aspect of eucharistic doctrine. There can be no repetition of Calvary. The Lamb has seven horns and seven eyes, the horns relating to conquest and the eyes to spiritual gifts—again reminding us of the passages in Genesis and Isaiah, but also referring to Zechariah 3 and 4: "I will bring my servant the Branch. For behold, upon the stone that I have set before Joshua [Jesus] upon a single stone shall be seven facets [eyes]....They are the eyes of the Lord, which range through the whole earth." The seven eyes authenticate Jesus as the prophesied Branch. The Lamb, who is not yet seen enthroned in the vision, then approaches the one seated on the throne and takes the scroll, a direct parallel with the book-opening scene in Daniel 7. This signifies that judgment and revelation are placed in the hands of Christ. The worship of

the one on the throne is now transferred to the Lamb, thus proclaiming his divinity.

Then follows the second of the great heavenly hymns of
praise, within which the "prayers of the saints" (symbolized by
odors, incense) are included. (We should recall here the words
of the Psalmist which we sing at Vespers: "Let my prayer arise
in Your sight as incense.") The first hymn had declared that
God is worthy of power; this hymn now declares the Lamb to
be equally worthy. It is thus "a new song," celebrating the new
creation and declaring that the Lamb is worshiped as the Redeemer of all mankind. The redeemed are "from every tribe
and tongue and people and nation," and they have been made
"a kingdom and priests" unto God. Note that here again we
have antiphonal singing. The cherubim and the elders begin
the hymn, which is then taken up by the voices of "myriads of
myriads, and thousands of thousands" (echoing Daniel 7).
These are both square numbers, signifying "perfection," as we
shall again experience with the 144 of 144,000. Perhaps what
is being celebrated here is also the perfection of God's justice;
square numbers were also associated with justice. We still talk
today of a "square deal." The new creation is universal, and
thus we have all creation eventually joining in this great hymn
of praise addressed to the Lamb, thus linking the whole cos-
mos with the heavenly scene.

We can see in these two chapters, 4 and 5, a liturgical
development from the Jewish creation-liturgy to the
eucharistic liturgy of the Christian Church. God's new cre-
ative act of redemption in Christ is set out before us in terms
relating to both baptism and eucharist. It is presented as a cosmic event. It is not limited to a chosen people. It was in just
such terms that Isaiah had written of the Exodus revelation
(see Isaiah 43 and 51): "Thus says the Lord, your Redeemer,
the Holy One of Israel...who makes a way in the sea, and a path

in the mighty waters...Behold, I am doing a new thing...The wild beasts will honor me, the jackals and the ostriches...And the ransomed of the Lord shall return, and come to Zion with singing; everlasting joy shall be upon their heads...and sorrow and sighing shall flee away." The final phrase is taken up by St John in 7:17 with the idea of wiping away all tears.

We now turn to the seven unsealings which follow and which are of particular interest. The first four unsealings reveal the four horsemen. The colors of their four horses are: the first white, the second red, the third black, and the fourth pale (literally, "livid," possibly signifying "dappled" or "bay"), signifying respectively conquest, slaughter, famine, and death. Some commentators have seen the rider on the white horse as a figure of Christ, because of the color of the mount and because it is said that he was given a conqueror's crown. But this interpretation must be wrong, since in verse 8 we are told that power is given to them to "kill with sword, and with famine, and with pestilence, and the wild beasts of the earth." This implies that the four horsemen must be considered as a group. We cannot single out the first and place him in a different category from the rest. St John is here taking up both Zechariah and Ezekiel. We find the horsemen and their colored mounts in chapter 1 of Zechariah; and in Chapter 6 we find the colored horses drawing four chariots, traditionally symbols of the four winds. We should not be surprised, therefore, when we find the four winds introduced in the Apocalypse at the beginning of chapter 7. The sword, famine, and pestilence are the traditional list of the three plagues of God's wrath, which we find in Ezekiel 6; and in Ezekiel 14 we read of God's judgments upon Jerusalem in the forms of the sword, famine, the noisome beast, and pestilence, together with the promise that a remnant shall be spared—another important theme in the Apocalypse. It is possible to understand "the beasts of the earth" as a reference to the beasts who tore Christians to death in the arenas of Rome. We can be sure that the rider on the white horse is not Christ, but rather a parody of Christ. This is the first intimation of the antichrist, the one who appears to many to be Christ, but is in fact the enemy of Christ and the Church.

The fifth unsealing introduces the cries of the martyrs "How long?" precisely echoing the angel's question which follows the appearance of the four horsemen in Zechariah 1. The sixth reveals cosmic disasters clearly echoing the Synoptic Apocalypse, where Christ is speaking of the disasters which will precede His coming: "the sun will be darkened, and the moon will not give its light, and the stars will fall from heaven, and the powers of the heavens shall be shaken"— surely a prophecy which today we cannot merely shrug off as "purely symbolic." These are said to be "the wrath of the Lamb," and one must note the way in which "the wrath of God," which is here also "the wrath of the Lamb," should be interpreted, namely as the inevitable consequences which man brings upon himself. Then we are told of the four winds, initially held back by angels in order that the servants of God, 144,000, 144 a square number again, may be sealed on their foreheads. Sealing refers to Christian baptism and chrismation, of which Jewish circumcision was the type. This passage parallels that in Ezekiel 9 where God instructs that a mark shall be put on the foreheads of the penitents in Jerusalem before the executioners appear. It may also be an allusion to the mark of the Passover Lamb in Exodus 12.

Two significant points here are the order in which the tribes of Israel are given: Judah is named first instead of Reuben (now named second); and Dan is replaced by Manasses (one of the two heirs of Joseph). Judah is first, because Christ has been identified with the Lion of Judah. Dan is replaced, probably because of its dubious reputation (as seen in Genesis 49, where it is said that "Dan shall be a serpent in the way, a viper by the path"). We can detect here an oblique reference to Judas, the traitorous apostle who was replaced. There is a tradition that the antichrist will come from the tribe of Dan. In chapter 21, we find the apostles' names, written on the gates of the Holy City alongside those of the tribes. Judas' name would not appear there, so Dan's does not appear here.

Note that, at 7:14, the great tribulation is mentioned as if it were a past event, though in the sequence of visions it is yet to be revealed. The winds are still held back at this point. St John has therefore been given a vision of the ultimate hymn of praise sung by those who triumph through martyrdom. This is just one of several examples of the danger of interpreting the Apocalypse as a presentation of a strict sequence of eschatological events.

At 8:1, we have the seventh unsealing and the "silence in heaven." There has been much speculation on the meaning of this. It may indicate that the heavenly hymns of praise fall silent in order that the prayers of the suffering saints can be brought into prominence, in which case there is something of a parallel with the time of offering of incense in the daily sacrifice ritual in the Temple. It may, however, be a combination of two references: one to the original silence out of which the Word of God issued at creation, and the other to the silence which preceded the punishment of the Egyptians (see Wisdom 18 and 2 Esdras 7:30-34).

We now come to the seven trumpets and the disasters which each introduces. The winds, held back for the time of sealing, are now to be released. We may note, perhaps in reference to 8:10-11, that "Chernobyl" means "wormwood." Much was made of this at the time of the Chernobyl disaster. Wormwood is the star of the new Babylon, which by its worldliness and idolatry has poisoned the springs of its own life.

After the disasters heralded by the fourth trumpet, we have three "woes" introduced by the last three—note the 4-3 division that we have already mentioned. The sixth trumpet and its disasters take us to the end of chapter 9. We see that there is an intensification of the effects of these judgmental disasters. The "fourth" of 6:8 has become "a third" in 9:15. Note also that the first four fall on the sources of man's life, whereas the last three (the woes) fall on man himself, and appear to be explicitly demonic, as they are introduced after the falling of a star from heaven to earth, clearly a reference to a fallen angel. In 9:11 we encounter the one who is called "Abaddon" in Hebrew, but "Apollyon" in Greek, meaning "the one who destroys." It is possible that this is an oblique reference to those emperors who claimed to be incarnations of Apollo.

Chapter 10 introduces an interlude after the sixth trumpet, and we again encounter a scroll, though this time "a little scroll," and then in chapter 11 the mysterious figures of the two witnesses. The little scroll is explicitly linked with the sealed scroll of chapter 5 by the appearance of the "mighty angel," though it would appear from the word "little" that it does not contain everything that was in the sealed scroll. One possible explanation is that the sealed scroll contains the whole plan of God's purposes, whereas this little scroll includes only those parts of the plan which have been revealed through the Scripture to mankind. Some commentators have seen the sealed scroll as relating to the whole world while the little scroll is restricted to the history of the Church. The two witnesses have often been taken to be Moses and Elijah, representing the Law and the Prophets, the same two witnesses who appeared to the apostles at the Transfiguration. They can thus also be undertsood as signifying the dead and the living at the time of the Parousia (with which the Transfiguration is explicitly associated in Orthodox hymnology). Alternatively, they have been seen as Enoch and Elijah. In the context here, however, it seems more likely that they represent the Church's witness to the Gospel, two being the minimum required for valid witness, as is explicitly stated in Deuteronomy 19, and taken up in John 8:17-18: "In your law it is written that the testimony of two men is true; I bear witness to myself, and the Father who sent me bears witness to me." Notice the 42 months of 11:2 repeated as 1260 days in the next verse: this is three and one-half years, or the half-week of years!

At verse 14 we are prepared for the last woe. There has been a continuous building-up of horrors, and we would expect the seventh trumpet to announce some final horror surpassing all those that have gone before, yet it does not at first appear to do this. Instead, we are given a vision of the final victory and reign of Christ, and we hear another of the heavenly hymns of praise. Also, in chapter 12, we see the "woman clothed with the sun" (the Church) and the great red dragon (or serpent) waiting to devour her child. We are told of Satan's fall from heaven. A number of commentators have seen the woman as being the Mother of God, and, in a sense, they are right, because Mary is indeed the type of the Church. As the old Eve was the mother of the people of the old creation, so the Mother of God is the mother of all who belong to the new creation. The child is Christ. Mary with Christ in her womb can be seen as the type of the Church bringing forth a faithful remnant with the expectation of the Parousia, thus linking the two comings of Christ, in humility and in glory. One rather unusual interpretation here is that the woman represents the Jews, who in the last days will be converted.

The dragon has seven heads, in parody of the seven gifts of the Spirit, and hence has special reference to Satan working within the Church. It is at verse 12 that the third woe theme is picked up: "Woe to you, O earth and sea." Again, we should avoid the danger of simply reading through the text as if the events depicted are in a simple sequential order. The three and one-half years appear again in 12:6, and the three and one-half weeks in verse 14. This is the period for which the woman is said to be nourished in the wilderness, a clear allusion to the wilderness in which Israel was guided by the cloud and the fire, and was nourished with manna for 42 years. But there may also be a contemporary reference to the escape of the Jerusalem Church to Pella. Two flights by the woman into the wilderness are described in verses 6 and 14. These have been understood as flights from the world into prayer and meditation.

Let us now take some extracts from chapters 13 and 14, and then I will comment very briefly on them.

Chapter 13

[1]And I saw a beast rising out of the sea, with ten horns and seven heads, with ten diadems upon its horns and a blasphemous name upon its heads... [3]One of its heads seemed to have a mortal wound, but its mortal wound was healed, and the whole earth followed the beast with wonder. [4]Men worshiped the dragon, for he had given his authority to the beast, and they worshiped the beast, saying, "Who is like the beast, and who can fight against it? [5]And the beast was given a mouth uttering haughty and blasphemous words, and it was allowed to exercise authority for forty-two months; [6]it opened its mouth to utter blasphemies against God, blaspheming his name and his dwelling, that is, those who dwell in heaven. [7]Also it was allowed to make war on the saints and to conquer them. And authority was given it over every tribe and people and tongue and nation, [8]and all who dwell on earth will worship it, every one whose name has not been written before the foundation of the world in the book of life of the Lamb that was slain... [11]Then I saw another beast which rose out of the earth; it had two horns like a lamb, and it spoke like a dragon. [12]It exer-

cises all the authority of the first beast in its presence, and makes the earth and its inhabitants worship the first beast, whose mortal wound was healed... [16]Also it causes all, both small and great, both rich and poor, both free and slave, to be marked on the right hand or the forehead, [17]so that no one can buy or sell unless he has the mark, that is, the name of the beast or the number of its name. [18]This calls for wisdom: let him who has understanding reckon the number of the beast, for it is a human number, its number is six hundred and sixty-six.

Chapter 14

[1]Then I looked, and lo, on Mount Zion stood the Lamb, and with him a hundred and forty-four thousand who had his name and his Father's name written in their foreheads. [2]And I heard a voice from heaven like the sound of many waters and like the sound of loud thunder; the voice I heard was like the sound of harpers playing on their harps, [3]and they sing a new song before the throne and before the four living creatures and before the elders. No one could learn that song except the hundred and forty-four thousand who had been redeemed from the earth. [6]Then I saw another angel flying in midheaven, with an eternal gospel to proclaim to those who dwell on earth, to every nation and tribe and tongue and people; [7]and he said with a loud voice, "Fear God and give him glory, for the hour of his judgment has come; and worship him who made heaven and earth, the sea and the fountains of waters." [8]Another angel, a second, followed, saying, "Fallen, fallen is Babylon the great, she who made all nations drink the wine of her impure passion." [9]And another angel, a third, followed them, saying with a loud voice, "If any man worships the beast and its image, and receive a mark on his forehead or in his hand, [10]he also shall drink of the wine of God's wrath, poured unmixed into the cup of his anger, and he shall be tormented with fire and sulphur in the presence of the holy angels and in the presence of the Lamb. [11]And the smoke of their tor-

ment goes up for ever and ever; and they have no rest, day or night, these worshipers of the beast and its image, and whoever receives the mark of its name." [14]Then I looked, and lo, a white cloud, and seated on the cloud one like a son of man, with a golden crown on his head, and a sharp sickle in his hand. [15]And another angel came out of the temple, calling with a loud voice to him who sat upon the cloud, "Put in your sickle, and reap, for the hour to reap has come, for the harvest of the earth is fully ripe." [16]So he who sat upon the cloud swung his sickle on the earth, and the earth was reaped. [17]And another angel came out of the temple in heaven, and he too had a sharp sickle. [18]Then another angel came out from the altar, the angel who has power over fire, and he called with a loud voice to him that had the sharp sickle, "Put in your sickle, and gather the clusters of the vine of the earth; for its grapes are ripe." [19]So the angel swung his sickle on the earth and gathered the vintage of the earth, and threw it into the great wine press of the wrath of God.

The two beasts are antichrist—the great enemy of Christ and the Church—and his false prophet. The first beast is the personification of false christs and has ten horns; in Daniel 7 we find: "Behold, a fourth beast, terrible and dreadful and exceedingly strong...and it was different from all the beasts that were before it; and it had ten horns." Notice the parody of Christ in 13:3: there is a head that is mortally wounded but then healed—a parody of Christ's crucifixion and resurrection. Verse 8 concludes with a reference, and not the first, linking creation and redemption together, and reminding us that the Incarnation was part of the Father's plan of self-revelation from the beginning. The second beast, the false prophet and the personification of all false prophets, can be seen as a parody of the Holy Spirit. The two horns are a parody of true witness, and stand in contrast to the two true witnesses. The parody of

Christ is continued here as well, for this beast appears like a lamb; further, his servants bear his mark, a parody of the sealing. Notice that "It works great signs" and is "making fire come down from heaven" (vs 13). This has been seen by some as indicating that he will have all the marvels of modern science at his disposal. This entire passage points to the unholy alliance of the apostate church with the powers of the world.

This brings us to the number 666. The most obvious immediate reference is probably to Nero; but it is introduced with a call to wisdom, that is, to an understanding of its true significance. As I have mentioned already, there have been many attempts, because both Greek and Hebrew use letters for numbers, to identify specific persons with the number of antichrist, 666. We would do better to look for a general interpretation. If we remember that seven is the number of completeness, we can see 6 as the number of incompleteness and hence of evil, and specifically of evil masquerading as good. Six is almost 7, near enough to deceive "even the elect." The threefold repetition of the number 6 is therefore a parody of the Holy Trinity. It is probably also relevant to note that, for the Jews, world history was to run to seven millennia of which the sixth was to be the time of antichrist.

Chapters 14 to 19 are the final preparation for the general resurrection and the last judgment: the hymn of the 144,000, the seven last plagues of the bowls, the judgment of the great harlot, the fall of Babylon, and the destruction of the beast. First, in chapter 14, we see the true Lamb and his followers on Mount Zion in total contrast with the false lamb and his followers. It is as if we were being reminded that no matter what may happen on earth, the spiritual kingdom of the Lamb remains unshaken. We hear too of the proclamation of the true gospel of Christ in contrast with the false gospel of antichrist, a false/true theme which is encountered again as the harlot is contrasted with the bride, the apostate church with the true Church. Notice the connection of Babylon with the idea of impure passion [fornication] in verse 8. This may have an immediate reference to Rome, but its lasting significance is to the corruption of the apostate church by the world. Note too that in the final verses of this chapter there is reference to both the harvest and the vintage. That they are distinct is indicated by their association with two different angels, and it is significant that the vintage is crushed in the winepress of God's wrath. This has been seen as a possible reference to the two resurrections, the resurrection of the saints and the general resurrection and judgment.

After another hymn of praise, chapter 15 leads us into the seven last plagues contained in the seven bowls. We will pass over these and move on to chapter 17, merely nothing that, though in some sense with the bowls there is a recapitulation of what has gone before, there is now a new focus, namely the doom of the harlot, the triumph of the bride, and the coming of the Bridegroom. The doom of the harlot who has committed fornication with the kings of the earth is described in chapter 17. She has on her forehead a mysterious name; one which contrasts totally with the name promised to those who overcome. Her name is "Babylon the Great, mother of harlots and of earth's abominations," and she is "drunk with the blood of the saints, and the blood of the martyrs of Jesus." Again, there is the obvious contemporary reference to Rome, but there is also the continuing interpretation of Babylon as the symbol of adultery with the world, breaking the baptismal covenant, corrupting the faith, and profaning God's Name, precisely the characteristics of the apostate church of antichrist. Note that in verse 8 we have reference to the beast which "was, and is not, and is to ascend," a parody of Him "who is and who was and who is to come," the title of God in 1:4. Again and again in parody form, we have this underlying "666" theme: that which appears to have the characteristics of God and righteousness in fact falls short, and thus becomes part of the empire of antichrist.

Chapter 18 deals exclusively with the fall of Babylon, the great city which antichrist has constructed out of apostasy in the Church. Chapter 19 introduces the coming of the Bridegroom, the marriage supper of the Lamb, and the final destruction of the beast and his false prophet. It is the great climax of Christian eschatology. Here, in verse 11, we again encounter a white horse, but on this occasion there is no doubt that its rider is Christ, since he is called "faithful and true" (echoing the witness who addressed the Laodiceans), and a little later "The Word of God." He is also the one out of whose mouth proceeds the sharp sword (vs. 15) and on whom is written the name "King of kings and Lord of lords."

Now we come in chapter 20 to the text on the millennium and the subsequent loosing of Satan, perhaps the one great problem of the Apocalypse. Let us read the whole chapter, as it also includes specific reference to a "first resurrection" and to "the second death."

Chapter 20

¹Then I saw an angel coming down from heaven, holding in his hand the key of the bottomless pit and a great chain. ²And he seized the dragon, that ancient serpent, who is the Devil and Satan, and bound him for a thousand years, ³and threw him into the pit, and shut it and sealed it over him, that he should deceive the nations no more, till the thousand years were ended. After that he must be loosed for a little while. ⁴Then I saw thrones, and seated on them were those to whom judgment was committed. Also I saw the souls of those who had been beheaded for their testimony to Jesus and for the word of God, and who had not worshiped the beast or its image and had not received its mark on their foreheads or their

hands. They came to life, and reigned with Christ a thousand years. [5]The rest of the dead did not come to life until the thousand years were ended. This is the first resurrection. [6]Blessed and holy is he who shares in the first resurrection! Over such the second death has no power, but they shall be priests of God and of Christ, and they shall reign with him a thousand years. [7]And when the thousand years are ended, Satan will be loosed from his prison [8]and will come out to deceive the nations which are at the four corners of the earth, that is, Gog and Magog, to gather them for battle; their number is like the sand of the sea. [9]And they marched up over the broad earth and surrounded the camp of the saints and the beloved city; but fire came down from heaven and consumed them, [10]and the devil who had deceived them was thrown into the lake of fire and sulphur where the beast and the false prophet were, and they will be tormented day and night for ever and ever. [11]Then I saw a great white throne, and him who sat upon it; from his presence earth and sky fled away, and no place was found for them. [12]And I saw the dead, great and small, standing before the throne, and books were opened. Also another book was opened, which is the book of life. And the dead were judged by what was written in the book, by what they had done. [13]And the sea gave up the dead in it, Death and Hades gave up the dead in them, and all were judged by what they had done. [14]Then Death and Hades were thrown into the lake of fire. This is the second death, the lake of fire; [15]and if anyone's name was not found written in the book of life, he was thrown into the lake of fire.

We must avoid a literal interpretation of the "thousand years." We are not here in time as we understand it, but in eschatological time. We have seen the destruction of antichrist, his false prophet, and his empire (an alliance of the apostate church with worldly powers). But these events have taken place on earth: antichrist has been destroyed, but not Satan.

Satan's earthly henchmen have gone, but Satan himself remains. This parallels Daniel 7, where we find the beasts' dominion taken away but their lives "prolonged for a season and
a time." Thus, Satan as a spiritual power has yet to be destroyed. There is still the battle with Gog and Magog. The millennium can therefore be seen as standing for the victory
which has been achieved over all the earthly manifestations of
Satanic power, and specifically over the beasts (antichrist and
the false prophet). Christ reigns, but as the Father's representative. He cannot hand over the kingdom to the Father until all
spiritual as well as earthly opposition to the Father's will has
been overcome. St John uses an established concept, the messianic kingdom, to indicate this. It was unusual to have the period of this kingdom defined precisely, though a period of 400
years is specified in 2 Esdras 7. The fact that St John alone
specifies a millennium (a thousand years) no less than six
times in verses 2-7 indicates that "thousand" has a particular
significance. The most likely explanation relates it to a restora-
tion of the old creation. A thousand years was to have been the
natural span of man's life, but Adam did not achieve this because he had disobeyed the commandment of God. In Genesis
5, we are told that he lived to the age of 930, after which we
read of a general decrease in the human lifespans. So the millennium, the thousand years of the Apocalypse, can be interpreted as symbolic of the new creation in Christ, who, as
Redeemer, has restored man's primeval inheritance. Any interpretation of the millennium as literally a thousand years
within time thus leads inevitably to misunderstanding, even to
heresy, as indeed it has done so many times in the Church's
history. The expression "the first resurrection" refers to the
resurrection of the saints, following the pattern of St Paul's
teaching in 1 Corinthians and 1 Thessalonians which we read
in chapter 1: those who are "in Christ" rise first at His coming.

The "second death" refers to the final judgment after the general resurrection, the judgment on those whose names were not found written in the book of life.

In chapter 21, we see first the new heaven and earth and the Holy City. There is no more sea. Here "sea" refers to the chaos out of which the beasts have emerged. The first earth is said to have "passed away," but this does not mean "destroyed," but rather that its old form has passed away—it is now transfigured. This is important in view of the largely Protestant belief that matter has become intrinsically evil since the Fall, and that at the Parousia the world will therefore be utterly destroyed. On the contrary, we are given here the assurance that God does not destroy what He has created, but rather that all will be transformed and made perfect. In verse 5 we read that "He that sat upon the throne said, Behold I make all things new," a clear promise of the renewal of all creation. We then see the bride, the faithful Church, clothed with adornments representing the righteous deeds of the saints. This is in contrast with the harlot's adornments representing immorality and worldly luxury, the unrighteous deeds of the apostates. Note in verse 22 that the Holy City has no temple. In the Temple on earth it is the invisible God who is worshiped. Now that God's glory is visible throughout the whole renewed creation, a temple as such is no longer needed. The whole creation has become his temple.

In the final chapter of the Apocalypse, we see the vision of paradise regained. The curse of sin has been entirely removed, the last enemy, death, has been overcome. If there is no need of a temple, neither is there any need for the light of the sun or of the moon. The eschatological day has no night; it is perpetually bathed in the light of the Sun of Righteousness.

I would like to end with a passage taken from the epilogue, that is from verse 6 onwards of chapter 22. Reiterating: this remarkable book that we have examined is the most wonderful proclamation of the victory of Christ to be found in the New Testament. It is a proclamation that the victory of sacrificial love has already been won, and that we are each of us called to have a share in that victory. All that follows from that victory has not yet been worked out in the world. Evil still retains some of its power, but it has already been defeated. The triumph of righteousness is inevitable because, viewed spiritually, it is already accomplished. Of course, the book contains many warnings about the ultimate fate of those who choose not to be "in Christ." We each have this choice to make every day of our lives. Are we for Christ and his kingdom or for the things of this world?—that is, for Christ or for antichrist? As we shall see shortly, Christ promises to "come quickly," though it is hidden from us precisely what the word "quickly" means. It is important that we try to give it a spiritual rather than a purely temporal meaning. Certainly his coming in glory is sure, and we must always try to live as if it were to be today. At the same time, our spiritual life within the Church should be a perpetual experience of the Parousia (the presence) of Christ. Yet, we must always watch for the full manifestation of that Parousia at the close of the age. As St Peter warns us in his second epistle, we must beware of those who scoff saying, "Where is the promise of his coming?" Above all, we must never join their ranks, but remain with those who can truly say in their hearts, "Even so, come Lord Jesus."

Chapter 22

[6]And he said to me, "These words are trustworthy and true. And the Lord, the God of the spirits of the prophets, has sent his angel to show his servants what must soon take place..."   [10]And he said to me, "Do no seal up the words of the prophecy of this book, for the time is near... [12]Behold, I am coming soon, bringing my recompense, to repay every one for what he has done. [13]I am the Alpha and the Omega, the first and the last, the beginning

and the end." [14]Blessed are those who wash their robes, that they may have the right to the tree of life and that they may enter the city by the gates... [16]"I Jesus have sent my angel to you with this testimony for the churches. I am the root and the offspring of David, the bright and morning star." [17]The Spirit and the Bride say, "Come." And let him who hears say, "Come." And let him who is thirsty come, let him who desires take the water of life without price. [18]I warn every one who hears the words of the prophecy of this book: if any one adds to them, God will add to him the plagues described in this book, [19]and if any one takes away from the words of the book of this prophecy, God will take away his share in the tree of life and in the holy city, which are described in this book. [20]He who testifies to these things says, "Surely I am coming soon." Amen. Come, Lord Jesus! [21]The grace of our Lord Jesus Christ be with all the saints. Amen.

Maranatha—Lord, come!

A Short Bibliography

Archbishop Averky, *The Apocalypse of St John: An Orthodox Commentary* (Valaam Society of American/St Herman of Alaska Press, 1985, republished 1995).

Richard Baukham, *The Climax of Prophecy* (T & T Clark, 1993)

Austin Farrer, *The Revelation of St. John the Divine* (Oxford University Press, 1964).

Bishop Gerasimos of Abydos, *At the End of Time* (Holy Cross, 1997).

John Sweet, *Revelation* (SCM Pelican Commentaries, SCM Press, 1979).

G. R. Beasley-Murray, *The Book of Revelation*, New Century Bible Commentary (Eerdman's, 1974).

I. Beckwith, *The Apocalypse of John* (Macmillan, 1919).

E. W. Benson, *An Introductory Study of the Revelation of St John the Divine* (Macmillan, 1900).

G. B. Caird, *The Revelation of St John the Divine*, New Testament Commentaries (Black, Harper & Row, 1966).

P. Carrington, *The Meaning of Revelation* (SPCK, 1931).

R. H. Charles, *Revelation, vols. I and II*, International Critical Commentary (Clark & Scribner, 1920).

Roger W. Cowley, *The Traditional Interpretation of the Apocalypse of St John in the Ethiopian Orthodox Church* (Cambridge University Press, 1983).

George Eldon Ladd, *The Revelation of St John* (Eerdmans, 1972).

Leon Morris, *Revelation* (Inter-Varsity Press, 1969)

R. H. Preston & A. T. Hanson, *The Revelation of St John the Divine,* Torch Bible Commentaries (SCM & Macmillan, 1949).

P. Prigent, *Apocalypse et Liturgie* (Delachaux et Niestle, 1964).

H. H. Rowley, *The Relevance of Apocalyptic* (Lutterworth 1963).

H. B. Swete, *The Apocalypse of St John* (Macmillan, 1906).

Leonard L. Thompson, *The Book of Revelation* (Oxford 1990).

(None of the above can be unreservedly recommended.)

Some Topics for Discussion

1. The Apocalypse contains a number of liturgical hymns of praise, one or two of which have been identified. Which are the others?

2. We have encountered the "half-week" in the seals, the trumpets, etc. How is this concept used in the Apocalypse?

3. Can you find further passages in the letters justifying the claim that the last three letters mirror the first three?

4. A number of changes of scene have been identified whereby we pass from earth to heaven and back again. Can you identify others?

5. A number of commentators have argued for extensive overlapping in the Apocalypse. Discuss this claim with reference to the letters, seals, trumpets, and bowls.

6. Some eucharistic overtones have been suggested: can you identify other passages where there are clear eucharistic references?

7. It has been suggested that certain passages relate specifically to the history of the world, while others are confined to that of the Church. Discuss this.

8. At times John records "hearing," while elsewhere he records "seeing." Identify some examples and discuss if there is any special significance in distinguishing between them.

9. Compare the seven letters to the churches with the seven oracles of Amos 1-2.

10. It has been suggested that the themes of the letters can be seen as setting the themes in the remaining part of the Apocalypse. Discuss this with reference to the text.

11. In Rev. 7:17 there is reference to "living waters." Compare the various ways in which the words "sea" and "waters" are used in the Apocalypse.

12. In what ways are numbers used in the Apocalypse?
13. In what ways can the Apocalypse be said to represent both contemporary and future events?
14. What sequence of events leading to the final judgment appears to be foretold in the Apocalypse?
15. Examine the ways the faithful Church and the apostate church are represented in the Apocalypse.

The above questions are designed to make you return to the text of the Apocalypse and to study it more fully than has been possible so far. Try to give as complete and detailed responses as possible.

List of Scriptural Quotations

Ezekiel
1:4-2:2; 2:9-3:3
5:1-8, 12-end; 6:4-8; 7:23-8:4
9:4-6; 10:1-12, 14, 16-19
16:8-17, 23-32, 35-41
27:1-4; 28:3-8, 11-19
38:1-4, 8-9, 15-end; 39:4-7, 11-13, 21-24
40:2-6, 20, 24, 35; 43:1-2, 4-9; 47:1-2, 8-9; 48:30-end

Daniel
2:31-44
7:1-27
8:3-26
12:1-9, 12-end

Matthew
24:3-31, 36-44; 25:31-33, 46

Paul
1 Cor 15:12-28, 35-57
1 Thess 4:13-5:6
2 Thess 2:1-12

2 Peter
3:3-14

1 John
2:18-22, 3:2-3

Apocalypse
1:1-3
1:4-11
1:12-20
2:1-7
4:1-end
5:1-end
13:1, 4-8, 11-12, 16-end; 14:1-3, 6-11, 14-19
20:1-end
22:6, 10, 12-14, 16-end